Gandhi: A Very Short Introduction

Very Short Introductions available now:

ACCOUNTING Christopher Nobes
ADVERTISING Winston Fletcher
AFRICAN HISTORY
    John Parker and Richard Rathbone
AGNOSTICISM Robin Le Poidevin
ALEXANDER THE GREAT Hugh Bowden
AMERICAN HISTORY Paul S. Boyer
AMERICAN IMMIGRATION David A. Gerber
AMERICAN POLITICAL PARTIES AND
    ELECTIONS L. Sandy Maisel
AMERICAN POLITICS Richard M. Valelly
THE AMERICAN PRESIDENCY Charles O. Jones
ANAESTHESIA Aidan O'Donnell
ANARCHISM Colin Ward
ANCIENT EGYPT Ian Shaw
ANCIENT GREECE Paul Cartledge
THE ANCIENT NEAR EAST Amanda H. Podany
ANCIENT PHILOSOPHY Julia Annas
ANCIENT WARFARE Harry Sidebottom
ANGELS David Albert Jones
ANGLICANISM Mark Chapman
THE ANGLO-SAXON AGE John Blair
THE ANIMAL KINGDOM Peter Holland
ANIMAL RIGHTS David DeGrazia
THE ANTARCTIC Klaus Dodds
ANTISEMITISM Steven Beller
ANXIETY Daniel Freeman and Jason Freeman
THE APOCRYPHAL GOSPELS Paul Foster
ARCHAEOLOGY Paul Bahn
ARCHITECTURE Andrew Ballantyne
ARISTOCRACY William Doyle
ARISTOTLE Jonathan Barnes
ART HISTORY Dana Arnold
ART THEORY Cynthia Freeland
ASTROBIOLOGY David C. Catling
ATHEISM Julian Baggini
AUGUSTINE Henry Chadwick
AUSTRALIA Kenneth Morgan
AUTISM Uta Frith
THE AVANT GARDE David Cottington
THE AZTECS David Carrasco
BACTERIA Sebastian G. B. Amyes
BARTHES Jonathan Culler
THE BEATS David Sterritt
BEAUTY Roger Scruton
BESTSELLERS John Sutherland
THE BIBLE John Riches
BIBLICAL ARCHAEOLOGY Eric H. Cline
BIOGRAPHY Hermione Lee
THE BLUES Elijah Wald
THE BOOK OF MORMON Terryl Givens
BORDERS Alexander C. Diener and Joshua Hagen
THE BRAIN Michael O'Shea
THE BRITISH CONSTITUTION Martin Loughlin
THE BRITISH EMPIRE Ashley Jackson
BRITISH POLITICS Anthony Wright
BUDDHA Michael Carrithers
BUDDHISM Damien Keown
BUDDHIST ETHICS Damien Keown
CANCER Nicholas James
CAPITALISM James Fulcher
CATHOLICISM Gerald O'Collins
CAUSATION Stephen Mumford and Rani Lill Anjum
THE CELL Terence Allen and Graham Cowling
THE CELTS Barry Cunliffe
CHAOS Leonard Smith
CHILDREN'S LITERATURE Kimberley Reynolds

CHINESE LITERATURE Sabina Knight
CHOICE THEORY Michael Allingham
CHRISTIAN ART Beth Williamson
CHRISTIAN ETHICS D. Stephen Long
CHRISTIANITY Linda Woodhead
CITIZENSHIP Richard Bellamy
CIVIL ENGINEERING David Muir Wood
CLASSICAL LITERATURE William Allan
CLASSICAL MYTHOLOGY Helen Morales
CLASSICS Mary Beard and John Henderson
CLAUSEWITZ Michael Howard
CLIMATE Mark Maslin
THE COLD WAR Robert McMahon
COLONIAL AMERICA Alan Taylor
COLONIAL LATIN AMERICAN
    LITERATURE Rolena Adorno
COMEDY Matthew Bevis
COMMUNISM Leslie Holmes
COMPLEXITY John H. Holland
THE COMPUTER Darrel Ince
THE CONQUISTADORS Matthew Restall and
    Felipe Fernández-Armesto
CONSCIENCE Paul Strohm
CONSCIOUSNESS Susan Blackmore
CONTEMPORARY ART Julian Stallabrass
CONTEMPORARY FICTION Robert Eaglestone
CONTINENTAL PHILOSOPHY Simon Critchley
CORAL REEFS Charles Sheppard
COSMOLOGY Peter Coles
CRITICAL THEORY Stephen Eric Bronner
THE CRUSADES Christopher Tyerman
CRYPTOGRAPHY Fred Piper and Sean Murphy
THE CULTURAL REVOLUTION
    Richard Curt Kraus
DADA AND SURREALISM David Hopkins
DARWIN Jonathan Howard
THE DEAD SEA SCROLLS Timothy Lim
DEMOCRACY Bernard Crick
DERRIDA Simon Glendinning
DESCARTES Tom Sorell
DESERTS Nick Middleton
DESIGN John Heskett
DEVELOPMENTAL BIOLOGY Lewis Wolpert
THE DEVIL Darren Oldridge
DIASPORA Kevin Kenny
DICTIONARIES Lynda Mugglestone
DINOSAURS David Norman
DIPLOMACY Joseph M. Siracusa
DOCUMENTARY FILM Patricia Aufderheide
DREAMING J. Allan Hobson
DRUGS Leslie Iversen
DRUIDS Barry Cunliffe
EARLY MUSIC Thomas Forrest Kelly
THE EARTH Martin Redfern
ECONOMICS Partha Dasgupta
EDUCATION Gary Thomas
EGYPTIAN MYTH Geraldine Pinch
EIGHTEENTH-CENTURY BRITAIN Paul Langford
THE ELEMENTS Philip Ball
EMOTION Dylan Evans
EMPIRE Stephen Howe
ENGELS Terrell Carver
ENGINEERING David Blockley
ENGLISH LITERATURE Jonathan Bate
ENVIRONMENTAL ECONOMICS Stephen Smith
EPIDEMIOLOGY Rodolfo Saracci
ETHICS Simon Blackburn

Bhikhu Parekh

GANDHI

A Very Short Introduction

OXFORD
UNIVERSITY PRESS

OXFORD

UNIVERSITY PRESS

Great Clarendon Street, Oxford OX2 6DP

Oxford University Press is a department of the University of Oxford.
It furthers the University's objective of excellence in research, scholarship,
and education by publishing worldwide in

Oxford New York

Auckland Bangkok Buenos Aires Cape Town Chennai
Dar es Salaam Delhi Hong Kong Istanbul Karachi Kolkata
Kuala Lumpur Madrid Melbourne Mexico City Mumbai Nairobi
São Paulo Shanghai Taipei Tokyo Toronto

Oxford is a registered trade mark of Oxford University Press
in the UK and in certain other countries

Published in the United States
by Oxford University Press Inc., New York

British Library Cataloguing in Publication Data
Data available

Library of Congress Cataloging in Publication Data
Data available
ISBN 978-0-19-285457-5

18

Typeset by RefineCatch Ltd, Bungay, Suffolk
Printed in Great Britain by
Ashford Colour Press, Gosport, Hampshire

Contents

Acknowledgements

I am most grateful to Pratap Mehta, Sudipta Kaviraj, Noel O'Sullivan, Judith Brown, and Terry McNeill for their valuable comments on the whole or parts of this book. Terry McNeill additionally ensured a happy academic environment in which to work. Pratap Mehta and Sudipta Kaviraj, whose knowledge of the Indian philosophical tradition is greater than mine, alerted me to issues I would otherwise have overlooked. During our 35 years of friendship Noel O'Sullivan has influenced my thinking in ways I cannot easily identify, and for which I thank him warmly. Fred Dallmayr, Anthony Parel, Thomas Pantham, Leroy Rouner, Meghnad Desai, Homi Bhabha, the late and much missed Ushaben Mehta, Ronald Terchek, and Usha Thakkar have placed me in their debt by discussing my ideas on Gandhi with me over many years. I owe thanks to Sir Keith Thomas and Rebecca Hunt for their helpful comments on the final draft, and to my brother Chandrakant Shroff and to C. B. Patel for their friendship and kindness over the years. I thank Sue Wiles for typing the book and Amalendu Misra for preparing the index.

I dedicate the book to the victims of intercommunal violence in India, and to my good friend Lakshmi Mal Singhvi who in his quiet way has done much to promote religious harmony.

This book first appeared under the title *Gandhi* in the Past Masters Series of Oxford University Press. As it now appears in a new series, I've made a few changes in the text, many of them minor and largely stylistic. The book is different enough to be a new entity, yet sufficiently similar to the old to count as its reincarnation.

List of illustrations

Abbreviations

The Collected Works of Mahatma Gandhi, 90 volumes (New Delhi: Publications Division of the Government of India, 1958–84) are cited by volume number and page.

A   *An Autobiography: The Story of my Experiments with Truth*, tr. Mahadev Desai (London: Jonathan Cape, 1966).

B   Judith Brown, *Gandhi: Prisoner of Hope* (London: Yale University Press, 1991).

F   Louis Fischer, *Gandhi: His Life and Message for the World* (New York: New American Library, 1954).

G   Louis Fischer, *The Life of Mahatma Gandhi* (Bombay: Bharatiya Vidya Bhavan, 4th combined edition, 1983).

K   Martin Luther King, Jr, *Stride towards Freedom: The Montgomery Story* (New York: Harper & Row, 1958).

M   *The Moral and Political Writings of Mahatma Gandhi*, ed. Raghavan Iyer, 3 volumes (Oxford: Clarendon Press, 1986).

All the Sanskrit and Hindi words used in the book are defined in the Glossary.

Chapter 1
Life and work

Mohandas Karamchand Gandhi was born in 1869 in the coastal town of Porbandar, one of scores of tiny princely states and now part of the Indian state of Gujarat. Although the Gandhis, meaning grocers, were merchants by caste, they had risen to important political positions. Mohandas's father was the chief administrator and member of the court of Porbandar, and his grandfather that of the adjacent tiny state of Junagadh.

Gandhi grew up in an eclectic religious environment. His parents were followers of the largely devotional Hindu cult of Vishnu (or Vaishnavites). His mother belonged to the Pranami sect, which combined Hindu and Muslim religious beliefs, gave equal honour to the sacred books of the Vaishnavites and the Koran, and preached religious harmony. Her religious fasts and vows, observed without exception all her life, left an abiding impression on her son. His father's friends included many Jains who preached a strict doctrine of non-violence and self-discipline. Gandhi was also exposed to Christian missionaries, but Christianity was not a significant presence in his childhood. Like many Hindus he unselfconsciously imbibed a variety of religious beliefs, but had no deep knowledge of any religious tradition including his own.

Gandhi was a shy and mediocre student, and completed his school

1. Gandhi in 1942

education with average results. He was married to Kasturbai when they were both 13 years of age, an experience that turned him into a bitter enemy of child marriage. Sex understandably obsessed him greatly in his early years. One night when he was 16 years of age, he left his dying father to spend some time with his wife. His father's death during his short absence hurt him deeply. Although many commentators have used this incident to explain his hostility to sex, there is little real evidence to support this view. In his autobiography Gandhi only said the incident created a deep sense of 'shame' in him. What is more, he continued to enjoy his wife's company for several years afterwards and went on to raise four sons. He did not become seriously interested in celibacy until nearly 16 years after the incident and, although the sense of guilt played a part, his real reason was a desire to conserve his physical and spiritual energies for the important political struggles on which he had then embarked.

Gandhi left for England in 1888 to train as a lawyer, after giving a pledge to his mother that he would avoid wine, women, and meat. In the early months he lived the life of an English gentleman, buying himself a morning suit, a top hat, and a silver-headed cane, and taking lessons in dancing, elocution, and the violin. As the money ran out and after he had narrowly escaped a sexual temptation, better sense prevailed, and Gandhi turned to the more serious aspects of English life. Like many other colonial leaders he discovered the West and the East at more or less the same time, and one through the other. He read widely about British and European law and politics, interacted with theosophists, and studied Christianity, finding the Old Testament somewhat disagreeable but the New deeply moving. He also read about his own religious tradition, especially the *Gita* and Edwin Arnold's *Light of Asia*, which respectively initiated him into the Hindu and Buddhist philosophies. Gandhi was called to the bar in June 1891 and left for India two days later.

Gandhi's legal career in India was disappointing. He was too shy to open

2. Gandhi as a law student in London in 1890

his mouth in court and had to give away his first barrister's brief to a colleague. He turned to drafting applications and managed to make ends meet. However, the work did not interest him much, and it also exposed him to court intrigues which he found tiresome. When a Muslim firm in South Africa sought his services as a lawyer and a correspondence clerk, Gandhi readily accepted the offer. He sailed for South Africa in 1893 intending to spend a year there but instead stayed on for 21 years.

South Africa

South Africa was a turning point in Gandhi's life. It confronted him with many unusual experiences and challenges, and profoundly transformed him. Within a week of his arrival he had an experience that changed the course of his life. When travelling from Durban to Pretoria, he was thrown out of a train in the middle of the night for daring to travel first-class, and spent the rest of the night shivering in the waiting room at Petermaritzburg station. The distraught Gandhi debated whether to return to India or stay on and fight for his rights, and resolved to do the latter. The next day he travelled to Charlestown without difficulty, but the driver of the stagecoach that carried him to Johannesburg refused to let him travel inside, and asked him to sit next to him. Gandhi reluctantly agreed. Later he was asked to move and sit on a mat on the floor. Smarting under a sense of injustice, he refused, whereupon the driver started beating him and tried to push him off the coach until his fellow passengers saved him. Some months later he was kicked into the gutter by a sentry for daring to walk past President Kruger's house in Pretoria (A 91–6).

Indians who had begun to migrate to South Africa from the 1860s as indentured labourers to work on sugar and coffee plantations suffered all kinds of indignities and discrimination, especially in Natal and Transvaal, where they were heavily concentrated. In April 1894, when Gandhi was about to return to India for good, the legislature of Natal was debating the Indian Franchise Bill, which would have taken away Indians' voting rights. Gandhi's Muslim employer urged him to stay on to lead the fight, and he readily agreed. He founded the Natal Indian Congress and his campaign succeeded in partially reducing the harshness of the Bill. His similar campaigns against immigration restrictions and discriminatory licensing laws were much less successful. He increasingly began to complain that constitutional pressures, petitions, and rational persuasion were making no impact on 'prejudiced' minds, and wondered what else he should do.

He found the answer a few years later. When Transvaal passed a law in 1907 requiring the registration and fingerprinting of all Indians and giving the police the power to enter their houses to ensure that the inhabitants were registered, Gandhi hit upon his well-known method of *satyāgraha*. It was a form of non-violent resistance and involved peaceful picketing of registration centres, burning registration cards, courting arrest, and gracefully accepting such punishment as was meted out. Gandhi's protest resulted in some concessions which, however, fell short of his original demands. It was followed by another *satyāgraha*, this time involving Indian women and miners, against such measures as the imposition of poll tax, the refusal to recognize Indian marriages, immigration regulations, and the system of indentured labour. This had greater success and led to the passage of the Indian Relief Act in 1914.

During his 21 years in South Africa, Gandhi's ways of thought and life underwent important changes. Indeed the two became inseparable for him. Thought came to have no meaning for him unless it was lived out, and life was shallow unless it reflected a carefully thought-out vision of life. Every time Gandhi came across a new idea, he asked if it was worth living up to. If not, he took no further interest in it. But if the answer was in the affirmative, he integrated it into his way of life, 'experimented' with its 'truth', and explored its moral logic. This approach deeply influenced his attitude to books. He read little, and only what was practically relevant. But when a book gripped his imagination, he meditated on it, brooded over its message, put its central ideas into action, and 'grew from truth to truth'. He mainly read religious and moral literature including Plato's *Apology* and William Salter's *Ethical Religion* (1889), the first of which he translated and the second summarized into his native Gujarati. Three books that influenced him deeply during his stay in South Africa were Henry Thoreau's *On the Duty of Civil Disobedience* (1847), a 'masterly treatise'; Tolstoy's *The Kingdom of God Is Within You* (1893), which 'overwhelmed' him and in which he claimed to have first discovered the doctrine of non-violence and love; and John Ruskin's *Unto this Last* (1862), whose 'magical influence' was a 'turning point' in his life (A 250). Inspired by Ruskin, Gandhi decided to live an austere life on a commune, at first on the Phoenix Farm in Natal and then on the Tolstoy Farm just outside Johannesburg.

> This book [*Unto this Last*] was impossible to lay aside, once I had begun it. I discovered some of the deepest conviction reflected in it. Johannesburg to Durban was a twenty-four hours' journey. The train reached there in the evening. I could not get any sleep that night. I determined to change my life in accordance with the ideals of the book.

During this period Gandhi embarked on a number of experiments involving diet, child-rearing, nature cure, and his personal and professional life. Under the influence of a medical book that greatly impressed him, he even delivered his fourth son himself. He became convinced that a political leader must be morally pure, and embarked on a programme of personal moral development. Constantly challenged by the ubiquitous Christian missionaries to explain and defend his religious beliefs convincingly or convert to Christianity, Gandhi often felt lost. The Hindu concepts of *ātman* (soul) and *moksha*

(liberation) puzzled him greatly, and he had to write to his mentor
Raichandbhai in India for clarification and guidance. Since Gandhi
learned about his religion in South Africa in a confrontational context
and without access to a rich and living Hindu tradition, his knowledge of
it was largely based on reading and reflection, and remained shallow
and abstract. Like many other things in his life, he made up his brand of
Hinduism as he went along, with all the attendant advantages and
disadvantages.

In South Africa Gandhi made close Jewish friends, one of whom
bought the 1,100-acre Tolstoy Farm for him, and acquired
considerable knowledge of the beliefs and practices of the only major
religion to which he had not hitherto been exposed. He called Jews
the 'untouchables of Christianity' whose persecution, like that of their
Hindu counterparts, was based on a deeply corrupted and gross
misreading of a great religion (lxviii. 137). Gandhi also cultivated close
Christian friends, especially the British missionary C. F. Andrews
(1871–1940), of whom he said that there was no one else to whom he
had a 'deeper attachment' (F 130). Under their influence Gandhi
renewed his study of Christianity and integrated several aspects of it
into his brand of increasingly redefined Hinduism, particularly the
idea of suffering love as exemplified in the image of crucifixion. The
image haunted him all his life and became the source of some of his
deepest passions. He wept before it when he visited the Vatican in
Rome in 1931; the bare walls of his Sevagram *āshram* made an
exception in favour of it; Isaac Watts's 'When I survey the wondrous
Cross', which offers a moving portrayal of Christ's sorrow and
sacrifice and ends with 'love so amazing, so divine, demands my soul,
my life, my all', was one of his favourite hymns; and in many dark
moments of his life he articulated his suffering in the image of Christ
on the Cross.

In South Africa Gandhi acquired political skills and learned lessons,
some of which served him well and others ill on his return to India. He

understood the value of journalism, and started and used the weekly *Indian Opinion* to propagate his ideas. He also saw how demoralized and incapable of concerted action his countrymen had become. Rather than fight for their rights, they expected others to do it for them and in the meantime circumvented discriminatory rules by bribing government officials. Not surprisingly he repeatedly rebuked them, urged them to 'rebel' against themselves, and warned them that 'those who behave like worms should not blame others for trampling upon them'. Gandhi also learned the art of self-projection and political networking. He wrote about his work to influential people abroad including Tolstoy, assiduously cultivated important Indian and British leaders, and ensured that his activities were well reported in India and Britain. In South Africa he had little difficulty uniting Hindu and Muslim traders, many of whom shared a common language and culture. He generalized this experience and both underestimated the distance between the two communities in India and exaggerated his own ability to bridge it.

Return to India

Gandhi had gone to South Africa an insecure, timid, and unsuccessful lawyer. He left it for India in 1914 a self-confident, proud, deeply religious, and well-known political leader. His reasons for leaving South Africa are not entirely clear. Although he thought and wrote otherwise, his successes there were rather limited and he must have known that he could not do much more. By contrast he had acquired quite a name and had established useful contacts in India, and might have thought that he had an important role to play there. Whatever his reasons, he returned home equipped with a new method of action and a long-meditated programme for India's regeneration. Gandhi was in those days an enthusiastic supporter of the British Empire. He thought it stood for great ideals with which he had rightly 'fallen in love', had given him unrestricted access to Britain and South Africa, and had exposed him to many new ways of life and thought. Not surprisingly he urged his countrymen in London and India to support the British war effort, he raised an ambulance corps in London in 1914, and recruited for the British army in India in 1918. Although a votary of non-violence, he insisted that his loyalty to the Empire required him to give it his full support in times of need.

After his arrival in India, Gandhi travelled throughout the country with 'his ears open and mouth shut', as his 'political guru' the great liberal leader Gopal Krishna Gokhale had advised him to do, to get to know the country he had left over two decades ago. His observations led him to two crucial conclusions. First, although independence was not yet on the agenda, there was considerable opposition to the increasingly oppressive colonial rule and a widespread demand for representative institutions. The 'begging' and 'demeaning' methods of the Indian National Congress, founded in 1885 and dominated by middle-class professionals, had proved ineffective, and the terrorist movement, whose spokesmen he had first encountered in London during his student days and with whom he had debated the ethics of violence during his subsequent visits, was gaining ground. Gandhi shared the latter's impatience and admired its courage and patriotism, but strongly disapproved of its violence on both moral and prudential grounds. Violence was inherently evil, not a viable option for a people who had been disarmed by the colonial rulers, and unlikely to build up moral courage, cultural self-confidence, and the capacity for concerted action among the masses. Gandhi thought that the method of *satyāgraha* that he had developed in South Africa was India's best hope.

Secondly, Gandhi's study of India convinced him of its 'degenerate' status. He had noticed it in South Africa and written about it in *Hind Swarāj*, his first book, in which he offered a systematic analysis of India's predicament and its resolution (M i. 199–264). Thanks to the centuries of foreign rule, Indians had become deeply divided, caste-ridden, conformist, fragmented, selfish, contentious, cowardly, demoralized, and lacking in a social conscience and civic virtues. Unless the country was revitalized and 'reborn', it could neither win nor sustain its independence. Accordingly, Gandhi worked out a comprehensive syllabus of national regeneration, which he appropriately called the Constructive Programme. Typically Gandhian in its content, it included both small and large items, covering different areas of life and some chosen largely for their symbolic value. It included such 'absolutely essential' proposals as Hindu–Muslim unity, the removal of untouchability, a ban on alcohol, the use of *khādi* (hand-spun cloth), the development of village industries, and craft-based education. It also included equality for women, health education, use of indigenous languages, adoption of a common national language, economic equality, building up peasants' and workers' organizations, integration of the tribal people into mainstream political and economic life, a detailed code of conduct for students, helping lepers and beggars, and cultivating respect for animals.

Although some of these proposals were rather trivial, none were without value. For example, the use of *khādi* was intended to provide a national uniform and create at least a measure of outward equality in a highly unequal society, to generate a sense of solidarity with the poor, to bring economic pressure to bear on the British government, and to reduce foreign imports. The use of regional languages was intended to bridge the vast and widening chasm between the masses and the Westernized elite, ensure cultural continuity, encourage authenticity of thought and action, and to forge indigenous tools of collective self-expression. The development of village industries was intended to help the poor in the villages, guarantee them gainful work, arrest migration to the cities, and, above all, to sustain what Gandhi took to be the necessary social and geographical basis of Indian civilization.

For Gandhi the well-planned *satyāgrahas* and the Constructive Programme, especially the latter, held the key to India's moral regeneration and political independence. For nearly 30 years he single-mindedly devoted all his energies to both. He needed a united team of men and women with complementary talents, and skilfully identified, nurtured, and welded them. Sometimes he took over whole families, used their members to reinforce each other's commitment to his cause, and even became their honorary senior member, resolving internal tensions and exercising considerable emotional influence especially over the women and the young. He skilfully linked various families and created a deeply bonded national network, with himself as its venerated head. Since he needed a journal to carry his message in his own words, he started and edited *Navajivan*, to which he later added *Harijan*. He required funds, and so he cultivated and shrewdly managed India's half a dozen richest industrialists. He needed to awaken and unite his countrymen, and so he initiated a series of well-planned *satyāgrahas*, each appealing to a clearly targeted constituency. He required a powerful political organization, and rebuilt the Indian National Congress from the bottom upwards.

Above all Gandhi needed to mobilize the masses. After long reflection and experimentation he evolved a distinct mode of discourse that was also a form of praxis. Convinced that human actions derived their emotional energy from the 'heart', which could only be addressed and activated by judiciously selected symbols, he evolved a powerful cluster of culturally evocative symbols including the spinning wheel, the *khādi*, the cow, and the 'Gandhi cap' (a white cotton cap popularized by him). The spinning wheel, for example, which Gandhi asked everyone to ply, served several symbolic purposes. It was a way of gently rebelling against modern technological civilization and affirming the dignity of India's rural way of life. It united the cities and the villages and the Westernized elite and the masses, and was an 'emblem of their fellowship'. The spinning wheel also established the dignity of manual labour and those engaged in it and challenged the traditional Indian culture which despised both. It symbolized social compassion, for those who did not need the proceeds of its products were urged to give away those products to the needy, an infinitely superior moral act to the patronizing donation of money. And it also forced the individual to be alone with himself and observe silence for at least some time during the day. Gandhi not only evolved countless symbols of this kind but also became one himself. Partly by conscious design and partly as spontaneous expressions of his whole way of life, his dress, language, mode of public speaking, food, bodily gestures, ways of sitting, walking, and talking, laughter, humour, and staff became symbols of a specific way of life. Each evoked deep cultural memories, spoke volumes, and conveyed highly complex messages.

Gandhi's symbols did not appeal to emotions alone, for he also offered a rational defence of them; neither were they mystical or arcane, for they were all drawn from the daily lives of ordinary Indians. They appealed to both the head and the heart, interests and cultural memories, the present and the past, and were designed to reach out to the 'whole being' of his countrymen and mobilize their moral energy. In their own ways they created a new aesthetics and a kind of private public world of discourse to which the colonial government had no access. No other leader before Gandhi had worked out such a clear, comprehensive, and powerful strategy of action, and none possessed either his massive self-confidence or his organizational and communicative skills. It was hardly surprising that he exercised unparalleled influence on Indian political life for nearly a quarter of a century.

For Gandhi the struggle for political independence had to be run in tandem with and subordinated to the larger struggle for Indian regeneration. If political independence became the sole or even the more important of the two goals, the country ran the risk of valuing political power for its own sake, encouraging careerism, giving greater prestige to office-holders than to grass-roots workers, and so on. Although Gandhi's view had its merits, it also created problems for him. The struggles for independence and moral regeneration had different logics and sometimes came into conflict; in addition, the struggle for independence involved both *satyāgrahas* and working within the representative institutions provided by the colonial state, and again these sometimes pulled in different directions. Many Indian leaders did not share the priority Gandhi gave to moral regeneration and the Constructive Programme, and took the opposite view that political independence was the necessary condition of moral regeneration and had to come first. While Gandhi judged a *satyāgraha* from the standpoint of its effect on Indian society and its regeneration, they judged it on the basis of how it affected conventional politics and furthered their demand for representative institutions. Furthermore, since Gandhi had not clearly worked out the relationship between conventional politics, *satyāgraha*, and the Constructive Programme, and since it had to be constantly redefined in the light of changing circumstances, his overall strategy remained somewhat incoherent, rendering his leadership occasionally erratic and unpredictable.

Gandhi knew this and sought to come to terms with it. He argued that different individuals had different talents and dispositions, and were suited for different kinds of work. Some felt most happy doing constructive work, others were happier participating in *satyāgrahas*, yet others were best suited for conventional politics. The political struggle should accommodate this plurality, and leave each individual free to do what he or she was best at. This both gave a sense of personal fulfilment and ensured the necessary division of labour, which the great task of Indian regeneration and independence required. As for himself, Gandhi said he felt most at home with constructive work and to a lesser extent with *satyāgraha*, and wholly ill at ease with conventional politics. He therefore concentrated on the first two, largely leaving the last to those suited for it. Although conventional politics could not be so easily disengaged from the other two, this was a sensible compromise and worked reasonably well. It also meant that Gandhi's relationship with the Congress remained loose and fluid. The Congress retained considerable autonomy and was never merely an instrument of his will; for his part he retained his freedom of action and was not just a Congress leader.

Although Gandhi's *satyāgrahas* in India followed the broad pattern of those in South Africa, he also introduced, as we shall see later, several changes to suit new circumstances and needs. The idea of fasting was one of them and became a subject of much debate throughout his life. For reasons to be discussed later, Gandhi had no doubt whatever that his fasts were not hunger-strikes, nor forms of moral or emotional blackmail, nor ways of evoking and exploiting others' pity, but forms of self-sacrifice and represented a perfectly moral method of action. His past experiences had convinced him that human actions sprang from 'both the head and the heart', and that individuals could not be shaken out of complacency on issues of vital moral importance by sermons and arguments alone. One had to touch their hearts and activate their consciences, and fasting was one of the most effective ways to do so. As Gandhi understood its nature and mechanism, the idea of fasting had two distinct sources, the Hindu practice of *tapas* (penance) and the predominantly Christian idea of suffering love. The fast was an act of self-imposed suffering designed both to purify oneself and to energize the consciences of those addressed by it.

Leadership of the Independence Movement

Thanks to his well-received work in South Africa and successful leadership of the Champaran and Kaira *satyāgrahas* of 1917 and 1918 respectively and of the Ahmedabad textile workers' strike of 1918, Gandhi became an influential national leader within four years of his return to India. His moralistic language, complex personality, clarity of vision, use of culturally suffused symbols, manners, enormous self-confidence, and courage to stand up to the established leadership both impressed and intrigued his countrymen, and added to his charisma. When the unpopular Rowlatt Acts, passed in March 1919 and directed primarily at 'revolutionary conspiracies', continued the wartime restrictions on civil liberties, Gandhi felt confident enough to launch his first national *satyāgraha* later that year, involving an effective nation-wide *hartāl* (cessation of work) and mass demonstrations. Contrary to his expectations, it was marred by cases of arson, looting, and violence against some Englishmen. Gandhi described it as his 'Himalayan miscalculation' and called it off, an action he was to repeat three years later in another context. The fear of public humiliation or losing his moral authority did not bother him in the least, for it was 'more honourable' to admit mistakes than to sacrifice one's principles, and in any case 'moral authority is never retained by attempting to hold onto it'.

Some violence still continued and the colonial government banned all public meetings in the Punjab. When one was held in Jallianwalla Bagh in Amritsar on 13 April 1919, Brigadier General Dyer ordered his troops to fire on the unarmed crowd without a prior warning, killing 379 people and wounding 1,137. The incident and the Hunter Commission's subsequent exoneration of Dyer discredited the colonial rule in the eyes of most Indians, and Gandhi wrote to the Viceroy that he could retain 'neither respect nor . . . affection' for the colonial government. A few months later he wrote three important articles declaring sedition a 'duty' and demanding an end to British rule.

Gandhi launched a Non-cooperation Movement in 1920, which lasted for about two years. It was inspired by the brilliantly simple but dangerous idea that, since the colonial state owed its continuance to the co-operation of its subjects, it would disintegrate if they withdrew their support and set up alternative institutions to fill the vacuum. Gandhi promised independence 'within a year' if non-cooperation was total and widespread. It was to be practised in several stages, and involved resignation from government services, refusal to use courts and schools and at a later stage to pay taxes and serve in the armed forces, and the burning of foreign cloth. Many were disturbed by Gandhi's proposal not only because they thought it unrealistic but also because of its anti-statist and quasi-anarchist implications. Gandhi rejoined that non-co-operation was a way of demonstrating the hollowness of the colonial state and the average Indian's complicity in it, and of reconstituting the new state on a popular basis. His idea of burning foreign cloth also provoked much unease, and some, including India's poet laureate Rabindranath Tagore, wondered if Gandhi was not stoking the flames of narrow nationalism and even xenophobia. Gandhi vehemently rejected the charge. Foreign cloth symbolized conspicuous display of wealth, 'infatuation' with things foreign, use of dress as a badge of Western identity, and economic domination by the colonial masters. To burn it was to 'purge' or 'purify' oneself of all this. It had the additional advantages of building up indigenous industries, fostering the cultural self-confidence of the masses, and hitting British economic interests (xxi. 102; xl. 84–5).

For his leadership of the Non-cooperation Movement, Gandhi was arrested and tried in March 1922. He characteristically subverted the trial by refusing to adhere to its logic. He did not hire a lawyer and faced the prosecutor alone, symbolizing the helplessness of subject India before a well-organized colonial state. He did not defend himself either, and not only pleaded guilty but also asked the judge to take into account some of the incriminatory material he had ignored. He turned his trial into a trial of colonial rule itself, using the occasion to explain why 'from a staunch loyalist and co-operator' he had 'become an uncompromising dis-affectionist and non-co-operator' and suggesting that there was something profoundly wrong with a system of rule which required incarceration of the likes of him. He ended by presenting the judge with a moral dilemma: if he approved of the prevailing system, he had a duty to inflict the 'severest penalty' on Gandhi; if he felt uneasy about the latter, he had a duty to condemn the system and resign (G 254–8).

The deeply moved British judge rose to the occasion. He bowed to Gandhi and remarked that he was in a 'different category from any person I've ever tried or am likely to have to try'. He reluctantly sentenced him to six years' imprisonment, saying that, if for some reason the government were to release him sooner, no one would be 'better pleased' than he. Gandhi responded by thanking the judge both for the most courteous manner in which he had treated him and for imposing a sentence that was 'as light as any judge' could have imposed under the circumstances. The trial, a remarkable episode in British colonial history, highlighted Gandhi's style of operation, the raj's capacity for decency, and the gentlemanly manner in which the two sometimes conducted their relations. Significantly, the colonial government never tried Gandhi again, though it did incarcerate him on several occasions.

The Non-cooperation Movement served notice on the raj and made political independence a widely shared national goal. It radicalized a large number of Indians, drew them into political life, and extended the organizational reach and social basis of the Congress. It also led to a large body of voluntary institutions, greatly expanded civic space, and reduced the moral hold of the colonial state. However, it failed in its basic objective of paralysing the colonial state by establishing an alternative one behind its back. It demanded sacrifices of careers only a few were willing to make, and implied a hostility to Western institutions that only a few shared. Not surprisingly students who had boycotted government schools began to return, lawyers resumed their practice, and an influential body of nationalist leaders insisted on participating in municipal, provincial, and national legislative bodies. Contrary to Gandhi's calculations, the movement unwittingly alienated many Muslims. Their middle classes did not wish to give up their hard-won careers or abandon colleges and universities. When Mohamed Ali tried to close down the Muslim college at Aligarh, he was beaten off by parents and trustees. Indeed many Muslims thought that Gandhi's plan was a Hindu conspiracy to hold back their progress!

Gandhi was released early from prison on grounds of health. He was elected President of the Congress in 1924, the only time he accepted a position within it. He was deeply worried about the growing separation between India's various communities, especially the Hindus and the

Muslims, which the Non-cooperation Movement had not only highlighted but also in some cases accentuated. His well-meaning but ill-advised support for the Muslim leaders' campaign against the British abolition of the Turkish Caliphate in 1919 had not promoted intercommunal unity either. Instead it strengthened the hold of the *ulemas*, alienated Mohamed Ali Jinnah and other secular Muslim leaders, encouraged pan-Islamism, and provoked Hindu suspicions of Muslim disloyalty. Gandhi now decided to tackle the question of Hindu–Muslim unity, and embarked on a 21-day fast in 1924 to create 'mutual respect and tolerance' between them. Apart from placing the subject high on the national agenda and encouraging some Hindu–Muslim cooperation, his fast achieved little.

Gandhi felt that he needed to concentrate on his Constructive Programme in order to build up the unity and self-confidence Indians needed to fight against the colonial rule and eventually to sustain their independence. He therefore turned to improving the status of women, removing untouchability, encouraging cottage industries, propagating the spinning wheel, and popularizing vernacular languages. He decided to observe a year of silence in 1926 and devote it to calm reflection, social work, and conserving his emotional energy. He had long believed in the regenerative power of silence and had for years observed Mondays as days of silence, communicating when unavoidable by notes scribbled with a pencil stub. As he wrote to B. C. Roy in May, 1928:

> I am biding my time, and you will find me leading the country in the field of politics when the country is ready. I have no false modesty about me. I am undoubtedly a politician in my own way, and I have a scheme for the country's freedom. But my time is not yet . . .

(CW, 36. p. 287)

Gandhi's time came in 1930. From the mid-1920s onwards terrorism and industrial strife were on the rise. The representative institutions established since 1919 had proved disappointing. Their powers were severely limited, and they were starved of resources. The deteriorating world economic situation affected India and led to considerable unrest. Gandhi felt that there was 'a lot of violence in the air' and that some form of civil disobedience was necessary not only because the situation demanded it but also to provide a safety valve for growing discontent and to avoid a split within the Congress itself. He was, however, worried that in the country's current mood even the most peaceful forms of disobedience ran the risk of turning violent. After 'furiously thinking day and night', Gandhi decided to launch a *satyāgraha* against the government's decision to tax salt in 1930. The protest involved breaking the law by making salt on the seashore. Officially it was to be his, not Congress's, *satyāgraha*, limited to himself and his carefully chosen associates, and involved a pledge by all that they accepted non-violence not just pragmatically but as an article of faith and would adhere to it even under the greatest provocation. Gandhi chose salt as an issue because it affected all Indians, united Hindus and Muslims, bore most heavily on the poor, and highlighted the inhumanity of the raj. Since the revenue it generated was marginal to the government, the protest was also unlikely to provoke harsh reprisals.

Along with 78 male companions representing various regions and religions, Gandhi, then 61 years of age, started his 24-day march south towards the coastal village of Dandi some 241 miles away. It was reminiscent of his five-day march into Transvaal in 1913 accompanied by a group of over 2,000 people. He covered between 10 and 15 miles a day, cheered and sometimes joined by hundreds of people from the surrounding villages, carrying copies of the *Gita* and quoting from both it and the Bible, and embarrassing the conscience of the Christian government by drawing a parallel between Gandhi's and Christ's confrontation with the authorities. With the whole of India urging him on and the world press reporting his daily progress, Gandhi finally reached Dandi on 5 April. With the consummate showmanship of a great political artist, he picked up a palmful of salt in open defiance of the government's ban. Along India's sea-coast and in its numerous inlets, thousands of people, mainly the peasants, followed his example and made salt illegally. They were beaten, sometimes brutally, and 60,000 of them including Gandhi were arrested and incarcerated for various lengths of time. The salt *satyāgraha* convinced Indians that colonial rule was vulnerable, and that they could end it if only they had the necessary will. It sent out a similar message to the British government. It demonstrated the inhumanity of the colonial government. And it also internationalized the Indian struggle for independence and exposed the British government to considerable world pressure.

The 1930 *satyāgraha* led to negotiations in London, where Gandhi arrived in September 1931, 17 years after his last visit. A popular and much sought-after figure, he met many leaders of opinion, Oxford academics, religious figures, and even George Bernard Shaw and Charlie Chaplin. He visited different parts of the country including Lancashire, where he apologized to the textile workers for the damage his boycott of British cloth had caused them and asked for their sympathetic understanding. He made a 'never to be forgotten' visit to C. P. Scott of the *Manchester Guardian*, 'the most impartial and the most honest paper in Great Britain' (xlviii. 433). He visited the King at Buckingham Palace dressed in his usual loincloth, which he had adopted in 1922 as a mark of his identification with the poor, throwing over his shoulders a shawl that he had worn in Britain to protect him against the cold. When a journalist commented on his sparse attire, he replied that 'the King had enough on for both of us'. When a year later Winston Churchill called him a 'half-naked *fakir*', Gandhi thanked him for the 'compliment' and wrote that 'he would love to be a naked *fakir* but was not one as yet' (F 565).

In the conference room itself Gandhi's impact was far more limited, partly because he was always ill at ease in formal gatherings, partly because he did not take the negotiations seriously, and partly because he was treated there not as the supreme representative of the Indian

3. Gandhi on the Salt March, 12 March 1930

people as he saw himself but as one of its several community leaders making equal claims on the British government's attention. The negotiations involved reconciling conflicting interests, and Gandhi found them somewhat tiresome. As they proceeded he realized yet again that, if India was to win its independence, he needed to win over its minority communities, especially the 'untouchables' and the Muslims. Both raised difficult problems, the latter far more than the former.

During the London negotiations, leaders of the 'untouchables' demanded a separate electorate of the kind enjoyed by Muslims since 1909 and Sikhs, Europeans, and others since 1919. It involved each community voting for its own representatives. Many colonial administrators, including the authors of the Montagu Chelmsford Report of 1918, had argued that separate electorates were 'divisive' and a 'very serious hindrance' to common citizenship, but the colonial government retained and kept extending them to earn minority loyalty and support. Gandhi protested against their extension to the 'untouchables' in the strongest terms both at the London conference and afterwards. In his view, unlike the other minorities, they were a part of Hindu society, and giving them a separate electorate would perpetuate their status as 'untouchables' and absolve the caste Hindus of their moral responsibility to fight against the practice of untouchability. Political calculations were not far from Gandhi's mind either, for the separate electorate would have reduced the numerical strength of the Hindu majority, encouraged minority alliances against it, and fragmented the country yet further. Gandhi did not mind reserved seats for the 'untouchables', for which all including the caste Hindus were to be able to vote, but he could not countenance separate electorates for them (li. 62–5, 116–20, 143–5).

When the British government ignored his protest and granted the separate electorate in the Communal Award of August 1932, Gandhi, who was then in prison, took the only course of action open to him, namely to embark on a fast. The 'untouchable' leader Babasaheb Ambedker condemned the fast as a 'political stunt', a 'vile and wicked act', but most Hindus including Tagore, otherwise a critic of fasting, thought it wholly justified. After five days of hard bargaining by Ambedker, a compromise was reached. The demand for a separate electorate was dropped, and in return the 'untouchables' received far more reserved seats than the Award had given them and special sums of money for their educational uplift. Gandhi realized that Hinduism was 'on the brink of an active volcano', and threw himself into his anti-untouchability work with greater zeal and commitment than before.

The last struggle

Hindu–Muslim relations did not have such a happy outcome. During the 1930s they were strained, but there was no cause for concern. Gandhi thought he had done much to bring the two communities together at the personal and political levels, and that things would improve once the colonial government with its policy of 'divide and rule' was out of the way. The Congress enjoyed support among the Muslim masses, and included several Muslim leaders of provincial and even national stature. The provincial elections of 1937 were crucial, especially as the 1935 Act had granted considerable autonomy to the provinces and was generally seen as paving the way for Indian independence. The Congress did very well in the general constituencies and, although it performed badly in Muslim constituencies, so did the Muslim League. The Congress formed ministries in all but four provinces.

The 1937 election results presented the Congress with both a challenge and an opportunity. It realized that Muslims were not behind it and should be won over, but also that they were not behind the League either and could be won over. Accordingly it launched a programme of 'mass contact' with a view to reassuring them that it posed no threat to their religious and other interests. The Muslim League read the situation in more or less the same way and launched a rather vicious campaign of its own, aimed at arousing Muslim fears and sense of insecurity. Realizing how much and how quickly the Muslim masses were becoming 'communalized', the Congress called off its programme and urged the League to make a reciprocal gesture. Jinnah, the leader of the League, not only refused to call off the campaign but intensified it.

Jinnah, Gandhi's greatest adversary, was a complex figure, and their relationship was full of strange paradoxes. Jinnah came from the same part of India as Gandhi, shared his language and culture, and was a lawyer like him. His family were first-generation Hindu converts. 'Jinnah' was a Hindu name and reflected the fairly common practice among Hindu converts of retaining part of their original name. Like Gandhi, Jinnah too adored Gokhale and regarded him as his political mentor. Like him, Jinnah had spent many years abroad. And although they worked out very different responses to India, both alike retained an outsider's perspective. Neither of them was intimately familiar with Indian history or his own religious tradition. Unlike Gandhi, Jinnah was not religious and strongly disapproved of the introduction of religion into politics. He had married a much younger Zoroastrian girl, enjoyed alcohol, and had no objection to pork. He knew Gandhi's charm and manner of establishing personal relationships, and carefully insulated himself against them. He spoke to him in English rather than their native Gujarati, shook hands with him rather than using the traditional Indian form of greeting with folded palms, and addressed him formally as 'Mr Gandhi' in preference to the more respectful 'Gandhiji'. Gandhi, who had succeeded in winning over or at least commanding the deepest respect of almost all his opponents, including such strong-minded leftist leaders as Subhas Bose and M. N. Roy, failed before a man who was closer to him in many respects than his other opponents.

Jinnah obviously could not mobilize the vast and illiterate Muslim masses without simplifying the political reality and offering them a naive and rather distorted conception of themselves and their place in

India. He introduced the language of religious nationalism and dramatically changed the character of the political debate. Hitherto he and the League had argued that the Muslims were a minority *community* entitled to a separate electorate and constitutional safeguards; they now began to argue that they were a *nation*, a distinct cultural and political unit entitled to full equality of status with the Hindus, and that India consisted of two nations. Although Jinnah was initially content to plead for their equality within a single state, the momentum of events soon got out of control and he became a strong advocate of the separate state of Pakistan.

During his negotiations with Jinnah, Gandhi challenged his two-nations theory. He argued that the language of nationalism was both inapplicable to India and inherently absurd. Unlike the European countries, India was not a nation but a civilization, which had over the centuries benefited from the contributions of different races and religions and was distinguished by its plurality, diversity, and tolerance. Hindus and Muslims, most of them Hindu converts, shared a common culture and, since even their religions had deeply influenced each other, they could not possibly be called separate nations. Furthermore, the very idea that each nation should have its own state was preposterous and impractical. In any case, the new state of Pakistan would include a large number of Hindus, even as India would include millions of Muslims. Since both states were bound to be multi-religious and had to find ways of accommodating minorities, there was no reason why an undivided India could not do the same. Gandhi told Jinnah that although he himself did not consider Pakistan a 'worthy ideal', he was prepared to accept it if Jinnah agreed to a plebiscite in Muslim majority areas. What in Gandhi's view Jinnah was not entitled to do was to arouse religious passions and threaten mass violence if he did not get his way (lxxii. 334).

Although the two-nations theory was untenable, Muslim fears were deep and genuine. Muslims had ruled over Hindus for centuries and feared reprisal or at least discrimination in independent India. The increasing use by Congress of socialist rhetoric frightened away Muslim landlords and upper classes, from whom many of the ardent advocates of Pakistan were drawn. The Congress had also missed the opportunity to win over Jinnah and the Muslim League during its period of office between 1937 and 1939, and to prevent an opportunistic alliance between the middle-class Muslims of which Jinnah was a spokesman and the feudal classes whom he had long loathed. It was this alliance that made Pakistan possible and at least partly explains its subsequent tragic history. Given more time, a more relaxed political environment, a less manipulative colonial government, and greater sensitivity and goodwill on the part of the Congress and Muslim leadership, ways could perhaps have been found to allay these fears. Under the circumstances many well-meaning constitutional schemes to keep the country together collapsed without a fair trial, and the much-dreaded partition of the country with all the attendant violence became inevitable.

While the bulk of Congress leadership came round to accepting the partition, Gandhi resisted it not because he was worried about India's territorial shrinkage but because he considered it a 'falsehood'. It denied a thousand years of Indian history and the basic spirit of Indian civilization, and rested on the inherently 'evil' principle of religious nationalism. He was also afraid that it would lead to much bloodshed and permanently sour the relations between the two countries. When he realized that the fast he had long threatened was likely to make matters worse, he gracefully accepted the partition and strove to create a climate that would both minimize violence and maximize future reconciliation. By and large he saw the partition in the image of the Hindu joint family. Those who could not live together were free to set up a separate household to avoid constant quarrels, but there was no reason why they should deny their shared history, hate and kill each other, reject cooperation on matters of common interest, and not aim at future reconciliation.

During the last few months of his life, Gandhi fought heroically against the corybantic wave of violence that had gripped most of north India. For many years past he had been plagued by profound political and spiritual doubts. He had often expressed anxiety about the future of India and the outcome of his personal, moral, and spiritual struggles, had even wondered if he was the right national leader and urged others to take over his burden, and had left Congress in 1934 to allow it to take decisions without being constrained by his towering presence (lviii. 404; B 284–9). Now he had no doubts about his course of action, for his duty could not be clearer. Knowing that the 'day of reckoning' that he had long feared had at last come, he decided, at the age of 77, to put his non-violence to the 'final test'. Everything he had stood for was at stake, and his very God was on trial. Since Gandhi had been loyal to God all his life, the latter would not let him down in his and his country's greatest hour of need. Gandhi now became a transcendental, God-possessed figure with no other mission than to tame the 'demon' of violence.

The personal and the political were inseparable for Gandhi. Every time he had faced a momentous political struggle in the past, he had turned inward to concentrate his being and summon up all his moral and spiritual energy. 'How can a damp matchstick kindle a log of wood?' (M ii. 69). The battle against the horrendous intercommunal violence required a more intense inner search than ever before. His religious faith dictated that good always triumphed over evil and that all violence dissolved in the presence of non-violence. The continuing violence had to be explained, and Gandhi characteristically blamed himself. God or cosmic energy was not working through him because of some deep inadequacy in him. Although he thought that he had eliminated all traces of violence in himself, he must be wrong. The only possible source of violence could be the presence of unconscious sexuality, for Gandhi a form of aggression. Accordingly he decided to put his celibacy to the severest test by embarking on the extraordinary experiment of sleeping naked with carefully chosen female associates, partly to flush out such residues of sexuality as might still remain, and partly to generate the immense energy he thought he needed to subdue the evil raging around him. The experiment generated great unease, and he wrote publicly about it. Although he was attacked, ridiculed, and shunned by some of his colleagues, he remained resolute. Just because his countrymen had made him a *Mahātma*, he was not prepared to conform to their expectations of him. His life was his and he had to follow truth as he saw it. If that meant losing his *Mahātma*-hood, he was only too happy to 'shed the burden'. Gandhi's experiments assured him that he was totally pure and that his God had not forsaken him.

In order to fight violence Gandhi had only one weapon left, his life, and only one way to use it, namely to make a sacrifice of it by means of well-calculated fasts designed to awaken the consciences and mobilize the moral energies of his misguided countrymen. In utter disregard of his physical safety and frequently murmuring 'kyā karoon, kyā karoon' (what shall I do? what shall I do?), he began his pilgrimage of peace to the Noakhali district of Bengal, the scene of the worst Hindu–Muslim violence (F 163–6). He stayed there from October 1946 to February 1947, walking from village to village, living in the huts of those willing to put him up, listening to their stories of atrocities, calming passions, and consoling the distressed and bereaved. He walked 18 hours a day and covered 49 villages. Sometimes his path was strewn with filth and brambles and, since as a pilgrim of peace he often walked barefoot, his feet became sore and developed chilblains. He had to cross bridges consisting of nothing more than loosely fastened bamboo poles, and sometimes he narrowly missed falling into the mud several feet below. There were also several threats on his life and a couple of violent scuffles. Undeterred, he continued his work, summoned up immense physical energy in his disintegrating body, and by the sheer force of his personality succeeded in restoring peace in Bengal and elsewhere.

When India became independent on 15 August 1947, Gandhi did not go to Delhi to participate in the celebrations or to unfurl the national flag,

4. Gandhi walking through the riot-torn areas of Noakhali, late 1946

and did not even send a message. He remained busy fighting violence several hundred miles away, and saw no reason for celebration. Soon after independence when Calcutta became the theatre of mass violence, Gandhi rushed to the city. When all his appeals failed, he began a fast unto death on 2 September 1947, just as he had done a few months earlier. Within three days he had performed a 'miracle'. Many who had been busy killing arrived at his bedside, wept at his tormented body, surrendered their weapons, and gave him a written undertaking that they would allow no more violence to occur, if need be at the cost of their lives. Lord Mountbatten was not exaggerating when he said that Gandhi had achieved single-handed what a body of 50,000 well-armed soldiers had failed to achieve in the Punjab. Gandhi saw no miracle, for it only confirmed his lifelong conviction that 'soul-force' was infinitely more powerful than the physical. And he needed no thanks, for his fast had given him 'ineffable joy' and a profound sense of 'inner peace' bordering on the experience of the divine (B 377–82).

From Calcutta Gandhi rushed to Delhi, where riots were raging. He visited Muslim areas and reassured their frightened residents. He also visited camps full of Hindu refugees from Pakistan who had lost all their possessions; some had lost their loved ones, and all were full of anti-Muslim hatred. Alone and unprotected, he consoled them, told them that there was 'no gain in returning evil for evil', and pleaded with them to show forgiveness. Angry and bitter Hindus sometimes broke up his multi-religious prayer meetings. Some objected to his recitations from the Koran and, since he would not compromise, the meetings sometimes ended abruptly. Gandhi even ventured into a meeting of 500 members of the RSS, a paramilitary body of Hindu militants, and warned them that their intolerance was 'killing' Hinduism. In order to shock the 'conscience of all' in both India and Pakistan, he commenced his last fast on 13 January 1948 to create 'real peace' in place of the deadly calm imposed by the troops, and to pressure the government of India not to renege on its solemn promise to transfer to Pakistan, which was then already at war with India, its share of collective assets.

Although many exasperated Hindus accused him of political naivety and pro-Muslim sympathies, most conceded that he was only being true to his principles and had nothing but India's stability and honour at heart. After five days Gandhi got what he had asked for. As he ended his fast, which was much admired in Pakistan, he feared for the two countries and broke down in tears. Gandhi's repeated triumphs against human savagery stunned his awestruck countrymen and made him a sublime and sanctified figure, an object of deepest pride and reverence even to those who were otherwise critical of his fasts and religious appeals. It was almost as if they felt that he had atoned for and redeemed them and lightened the burden of their shame and guilt.

Gandhi knew that violence was drawing closer to him. There had been several threats on his life; a bomb had been dropped at his prayer meeting 10 days before his death and he had refused to be frightened of 'a mere bomb'; he received abusive letters accusing him of appeasing Muslims and calling him 'Mohamed Gandhi'; 'Death to Gandhi' was a frequent chant at some of his meetings; and even his close friends showed impatience with him. He knew that he might be killed any day, but rejected all offers of protection. Indeed, it would seem that the violence had not only sapped his will to live but also created a positive desire to die a violent death in the hope that his death might achieve what his life had not. He evidently told his great-niece the night before his death that he should be called a 'true Mahātma' only if 'someone shot me and I boldly received his bullet in my bare chest without a murmur and while continuing to chant the name of Rama'. The following day a well-educated, highly articulate, modernist, and militant Hindu, who ideologically stood for almost all that Gandhi rejected, killed him after first bowing to him in reverence. Gandhi died instantly, allegedly murmuring '*hey Ram*'. His assassination on 30 January 1948 had a cathartic effect. It discredited Hindu extremists, chastened moderate Hindus, reassured the minorities, and pulled the mourning nation back from the brink of disaster.

5. Gandhi with Nehru in 1936

Gandhi survived Indian independence by just under six months. During that brief period when he was not busy fighting violence, he spent his time nurturing the Indian state and worrying about its future. He regularly advised Nehru, a secular socialist whom he had declared his 'political heir' several years earlier and who now was the Prime Minister of the country. He reconciled the growing differences between Nehru and some of his senior colleagues, urged his activist followers to leave Nehru alone to get on with the task of state-building, defended Nehru's departures from Gandhi's own ideals, and approved of sending troops to Kashmir. As for India's future course of action, Gandhi articulated his vision in terms of the tripartite strategy on which he had relied for nearly 30 years. The state was to be relatively autonomous and left in charge of those suited for conventional politics. The Congress, which had spearheaded the struggle for independence, was to dissolve itself and be reborn as a national organization pursuing the Constructive Programme, keeping a watchful eye on the state, and, when it acted unjustly, leading *satyāgrahas* against it. Since these were the tasks on which Gandhi had himself concentrated, he was in fact proposing that the Congress should institutionalize, preserve, and perpetuate his spirit. It spurned his advice, denying Gandhi's spirit an organizational incarnation.

Chapter 2
Religious thought

The cosmic spirit

Gandhi was a deeply religious thinker. Although he was profoundly
influenced by Hinduism, Christianity, and Jainism, his religious thought
cut across all of them and was in a class by itself. Belief in God was
obviously its basis. However, since Gandhi thought that the term 'God'
implied a being or a person, he preferred to use such terms as eternal
principle, supreme consciousness or intelligence, cosmic power, energy,
spirit, or *shakti*. Later in life he preferred to speak of *satya* (ultimate
reality or Truth), and regarded this as the 'only correct and fully
significant' description of God. Following Indian philosophical
traditions, he used the term *satya* to refer to the ultimate ground of
being, to what alone persists unchanged in the midst of change and
holds the universe together. For a long time he had said, 'God is Truth',
implying both that Truth was one of God's many properties and that the
concept of God was logically prior to that of Truth. In 1926 he reversed
the proposition and said, 'Truth is God'. He regarded this as one of his
most important discoveries and thought that it crystallized his years of
reflection. For him the new proposition had several advantages over the
old. It avoided anthropocentrism, and implied that the concept of Truth
was prior to that of God and that calling it God did not add anything
new to it. Since the sincere atheist too was in his own way seeking to
unravel the mystery of the universe and search for truth, the new

formulation provided the common basis for a dialogue between him and the believer. Gandhi knew many atheists with deep spiritual and even mystical feelings, and was anxious not to put them outside the pale of religious discourse (M i. 461, 566–92).

For Gandhi, Truth or cosmic spirit was beyond all qualities including the moral. As he put it, 'Fundamentally God is indescribable in words . . . The qualities we attribute to God with the purest of motives are true for us but fundamentally false' (L 200–2). And again, 'beyond the personal God there is a Formless Essence which our reason cannot comprehend'. Although the cosmic power was without qualities including personality, Gandhi argued that human beings often found it difficult to avoid personalizing it. The human mind was so used to the world of senses that it felt deeply disoriented when required to think in non-qualitative terms. Furthermore, human beings were not only thinking but also feeling beings, and the 'head' and the 'heart' had different requirements. The quality-free cosmic power or pure intelligence satisfied the head but was too remote, abstract, and detached to satisfy the heart. The heart required a being with a heart, one who aroused the deepest feelings and to whom one could become emotionally bonded, and required a personal God.

Gandhi articulated the nature of the cosmic spirit as follows. As one would expect in a man of action, he saw the cosmic spirit from the perspective of a life of action rather than contemplation. First, it was 'pure' or disembodied consciousness, not the consciousness of some being, for the latter would then have to be other than consciousness, but rather consciousness *simpliciter*. Secondly, it acted in a rational and orderly manner and was never arbitrary or capricious. Thirdly, it was active and represented infinite *shakti*, force, or energy. Fourthly, it pervaded, informed, and structured the universe. Fifthly, it was benevolent. Since the cosmic spirit is supposed to be beyond good and evil, it is not entirely clear what Gandhi meant by calling it benevolent. He seems to have thought that although it was beyond good and evil in the conventional moral sense, and although its actions were not amenable to moral evaluation, the fact that the universe functioned in a stable and rational manner, was conducive to the well-being of all living beings, and offered the necessary conditions for the good life showed that it had a structural bias towards good and was regulated by a well-meaning spirit. When its actions appeared cruel in human terms, as in the case of natural and social calamities, they should not be hastily judged but accepted as part of an incomprehensible but basically benevolent design. Sixthly, the cosmic power was 'mysterious' in the sense that, although human beings could acquire some knowledge of its nature and mode of operation, their knowledge was necessarily limited and tentative. Finally, although the cosmic power was omnipotent, it was subject to self-imposed limitations. Human freedom was one of them, and hence the cosmic power disposed but did not predetermine human beings to act in specific ways. Its omnipotence thus left space for human frailties, choices, and evil. For Gandhi evil was not an independent principle, but something 'permitted' or 'allowed' by the cosmic power.

Since the cosmic spirit was not a being or a person, Gandhi sometimes referred to it as 'it'. Since, however, it represented consciousness and intelligence, he also referred to it as 'He' (though never as 'She'). The distinctive nature of Gandhi's conception of cosmic power will become clearer if we compare it with the better-known Christian view of God. In its standard and popular version, the latter stresses his three features. First, God is an extra-cosmic being who pre-exists and is outside the universe. Second, he creates and imposes laws on the universe and ensures its orderly existence. Third, he is not only infinitely loving but also infinitely powerful, for to create and impose laws on the sun and the stars and the seas is obviously a dazzling and awe-inspiring display of power. The three features are closely related. As the creator of the universe, God is necessarily extra-cosmic, and power is obviously one of his most striking characteristics.

Gandhi viewed the cosmic spirit differently. Since the universe for him was eternal, the question was not one of creating but one of ordering and structuring it. His cosmic spirit was therefore not a creator but a principle of order, a supreme intelligence infusing and regulating the universe from within. Unlike a supreme being who can and perhaps must be extra-cosmic, a principle of order cannot be. Like most Indian thinkers, Gandhi was puzzled not so much by the material world as by living beings, not by the rhythmic and orderly movement of the stars and the seas but by the baffling phenomenon of life with its 'mysterious' origins, diverse forms, and their ingenious and complex mechanisms. God's awe-inspiring powers and dazzling feats did not interest or even impress him; in fact he thought that to stress them was to detract from God's true nature and inspire fear and awe rather than love and intimacy. Instead he stressed the cosmic spirit's intelligence, subtlety, skill, energy, and gentle and elusive manner of operation.

Gandhi agreed that the existence of the cosmic spirit was incapable of rational demonstration, but disagreed about the implications of this. By itself reason could not prove the existence of anything, not even chairs and tables; therefore, if it were to be the sole criterion of existence, we would have to deny the existence of the world itself. Furthermore, Gandhi could not see why only what satisfied reason should be deemed to exist. He rejected the view that it was the highest human faculty. If it was the highest because it said so, the argument was circular. As for the other faculties, they said no such thing. Reason was obviously an extremely important human faculty and should be assigned its due place in life, but it could not be made the sovereign arbiter of all others. Every belief must 'pass the test' of reason, but that did not mean that it could not transcend or go beyond it. Reason laid down the minimum not the maximum, and specified what we *may not* but not what we *must* believe.

Gandhi went further. Following the long line of Indian sages he argued that the existence of God was a matter of experiential certainty. Like many profound experiences in life, the experience of feeling God's presence did not come naturally to all. One needed to go through a long spiritual training and become a pure soul in order to qualify for the experience, and those who had done so had invariably spoken of 'feeling', 'seeing', or 'hearing' God. Gandhi claimed that his own life had borne out the truth of this. Since the existence of God could not by its very nature be rationally demonstrated, all that a believer could ask the sceptic to do was to undergo the required training and find things out for himself (M i. 504).

Gandhi agreed that to go beyond observation and reason was to enter the realm of faith, but saw nothing wrong in this. Human beings went beyond reason in most areas of life and could not live without faith, be it a faith in themselves, their family and friends, their ability to achieve difficult goals, or the belief that the sun would rise and the world would not come to an end tomorrow. Even hard-headed scientists relied on the faith that the universe was governed by laws, had a rational structure, and was amenable to human understanding. Although their faith was fully justified, it was none the less an act of faith and not a matter of rational demonstration. The important and the only legitimate question therefore was not whether but when faith was 'justified', and how to separate 'rational' from 'blind' faith.

Although Gandhi nowhere stated them clearly, he often invoked the following four criteria to determine when faith was rational or justified. First, it should relate to matters falling outside the purview of observation and reason. Whether or not elephants could fly or there was a cat in the next room was amenable to empirical verification and not a matter of faith. Second, faith should not contradict observation and reason. Third, since faith involved going beyond what could be observed and demonstrated, one must show that it was called for by, and had a basis or warrant in, experience. Finally, faith was a calculated gamble in situations where the available evidence was inconclusive, and was justified if it had beneficial consequences.

Gandhi contended that faith in the existence of the cosmic spirit satisfied all four criteria. The cosmic spirit lay outside the world of observation and rational demonstration, and belief in it not only did not contradict but was intimated and called for by human experience. The order and regularity of the universe could not be explained in terms of natural laws alone, for there was no obvious reason why the universe should be governed by laws at all and not be in perpetual chaos, or why it should be governed by laws that were stable and hospitable to life. Matter by itself could not create life, nor could its laws explain the sophisticated ways in which even the minutest living beings adjusted to their often hostile environment. Gandhi also found it mysterious that life persisted in the midst of destruction. Such destructive forces as earthquakes, floods, and storms could easily have snuffed it out a long time ago. Yet life had continued to persist, flourish, and throw up increasingly higher forms. Again, although both good and evil existed in the universe, good not only survived but also triumphed in the long run. In the short run and in individual cases, it might not, but 'if we take a long view, we shall see that it is not wickedness but goodness which rules the world'. Indeed, evil itself could not last unless sustained by good. Gangs of murderers might go about killing everyone in sight, but they must at least trust and help one another. Good was self-sufficient whereas evil was parasitic, and it was basic to life in a way that evil was not. The fact that the universe had a structural bias towards good and was not amoral could not be explained without postulating a cosmic spirit, Gandhi argued.

Turning now to the fourth criterion of rational faith, Gandhi contended that faith in the existence of the cosmic spirit was a better guide to life than its opposite. It made the tragedies of life easier to bear, encouraged human beings to care for and love one another, and guarded them against the cynicism provoked by the ingratitude and meanness of their fellows. It also helped them resist the temptation to bend moral rules to suit their narrow personal interests, inspired them to great acts of sacrifice, and gave them the strength to undertake actions and take risks they otherwise would not. Even if one did not feel *absolutely* certain of the existence of the cosmic spirit, belief in it had beneficial consequences and was a 'better hypothesis' than its opposite.

Unlike many believers, Gandhi advanced not the familiar strong thesis that there was an omnipotent God who created and presided over the universe, but a much weaker one that there was 'some' spiritual power who informed and 'gently' guided the universe. Even this weaker thesis, however attractive it might otherwise appear, is not without its difficulties. While claiming to take full account of reason, Gandhi assigned it a limited place and defined it in extremely narrow terms. So long as a belief was not patently absurd, it was deemed to be consistent with or permitted by reason. In this view there is no effective check on what beliefs one may hold, and even belief in ghosts and witches cannot be ruled out. On a more rigorous view of reason one might reach a different conclusion from Gandhi's. If one defined it in terms of the available body of scientific knowledge about the nature of the universe, belief in the existence of the cosmic spirit would appear problematic and certainly not as self-evident as Gandhi maintained. The order and regularity in the universe and the emergence of life can be explained without postulating the cosmic spirit, the alleged victory of good over evil in the natural and human world has only a limited basis in fact, and the pervasive violence of the natural and social world which Gandhi bemoaned is not easy to reconcile with a benevolent spirit. As for Gandhi's appeal to experiential certainty, it has a point but is not free of difficulties. The Buddha did all that Gandhi asks for, and evidently found nothing. What is more, one generally finds what one earnestly looks for and, if one does not, one could always be accused of not being pure or rigorous enough or of following a wrong regime of training.

Religion

For Gandhi religion represented the way human beings conceived and related to God. Since he postulated both impersonal and personal conceptions of God, he distinguished two different levels of religion. The 'formal', 'customary', 'organized', or 'historical' religions were based on distinct conceptions of God whom they reduced to the limited categories of the human mind and invested with anthropomorphic attributes. They involved prayer, worship, rituals, asking God for favours, and so on and were all sectarian. For Gandhi popular Hinduism, Islam, Christianity, Judaism, and all other religions belonged to this category. The 'true', 'pure', or 'eternal' religion transcended them. It dispensed with rituals, worship, and dogmas, and involved nothing more than a belief in the cosmic spirit and the commitment to realize it in all areas of one's life. Such a religion represented the purest form of spirituality and acknowledged that the divine was too complex to be fully grasped by any one religion. It 'transcended' but did not 'supersede' organized religions, which were all legitimate though limited articulations of it, and constituted their common 'basis' and connecting 'link'.

I do not want my house to be walled in on all sides and my windows to be stuffed. I want the cultures of all lands to be blown about my houses as freely as possible. But I refuse to be blown off my feet by any.

For Gandhi religion was concerned with how one lived, not what one believed; with a lived and living faith and not the 'dead bones of dogmas' (M i. 503). It had nothing to do with theology, which over-intellectualized religion, reduced it to a set of dogmas, and privileged belief over conduct. For Gandhi not theology but morality was the core of religion, and the latter was to be judged not by the philosophical coherence and subtlety of its system of beliefs as was argued by Christian missionaries, but by its ideals and the quality of life they inspired. As he put it:

Amongst agents of the many untruths that are propounded in the world one of the foremost is theology. I do not say that there is no demand for it. There is a demand in the world for many a questionable thing. But even those who have to do with theology as part of their work have to survive their theology. I know two good Christian friends who gave up theology and decided to live the gospel of Christ.

(M i. 517)

For Gandhi every major religion articulated a unique vision of God and emphasized his different attributes. The idea of God as loving Father and the concomitant emphasis on universal love, forgiveness, and uncomplaining suffering was most fully and movingly developed by Christianity. 'I cannot say that it is singular, or that it is not to be found in other religions. But the presentation is unique.' Austere and rigorous monotheism, the rejection of intermediaries between human beings and God, and the spirit of equality were 'most beautifully' articulated in Islam. The clear distinction between the impersonal and personal conceptions of God, the emphasis on non-attachment to the world while remaining active within it, the principle of the unity of all life, and the doctrine of non-violence were unique to Hinduism. For Gandhi every religion had a distinct moral and spiritual ethos and represented a wonderful and irreplaceable 'spiritual composition'. There was truth *in* each of them but that did not mean that they were all *true*, for they also contained some falsehood. Since each was unique, 'it is impossible to estimate the merits of various religions', let alone establish a hierarchy among them, in just the same way that it was impossible to compare and grade different artistic and musical traditions or great literary works (lxxv. 70).

Like many Indian thinkers, Gandhi was uneasy with the idea of revealed religion. He found the concept of revelation logically and morally problematic, the former because it presupposed that God was a person, the latter because it implied that he had favourites. God did give a helping hand to sincere seekers and guided them in moments of grave crisis – Gandhi claimed to have been a beneficiary of such guidance himself – but that was very different from the traditional concept of exhaustive divine self-revelation. For Gandhi, Jesus, Muhammad, Moses, and others were great spiritual explorers or 'scientists' who led exemplary lives, 'discovered' some of the profoundest truths about human existence, and received a measure of divine grace at critical moments in their lives; but they were neither perfect nor Sons of God or divine emissaries. God's revelation was available to all who became worthy of it by the quality of their lives, and largely took the form of practical guidance at critical moments.

Since God was infinite, and since the limited human mind could grasp only a 'fragment' of him and that too inadequately, every religion was necessarily partial and limited (M i. 478). This was equally true of those religions claiming to be directly revealed by him, for they were revealed to fallible human beings and embodied in an inherently inadequate human language. Religions therefore had much to offer each other and benefited from a sympathetic dialogue. The proper attitude to other religions was not one of toleration or even respect but *sadbhāva* (goodwill). Toleration implied that they were mistaken, though for various reasons one was willing to put up with them, and that one's own religion was 'true' and had nothing to learn from them; it thus smacked of 'spiritual arrogance' and 'condescension'. Respect was a more positive attitude, but it too implied both an unwillingness to learn from others and a desire to keep them at a safe distance. By contrast *sadbhāva* implied 'spiritual humility', a 'feel for other religions', and a willingness to see them flourish and learn from them.

For Gandhi, religion was the basis of life and shaped all one's activities. It could not be compartmentalized, reserved for special occasions or days of the week, or viewed as a preparation for another world. To be religious was to live in the constant presence of the cosmic spirit and to translate that awareness in all one did. It affected the smallest as well as the most momentous activities of one's life, including how one sat, talked, ate, and conducted one's personal, professional, and public life, and was nothing more than their 'sum total'. Since one lived out one's religious beliefs in all areas of life including the political, 'those who say that religion has nothing to do with politics do not know what religion means' (M i. 37–6). This did not imply theocracy or rejection of the secular state, for religion was a matter of freely and sincerely held beliefs and ruled out all forms of coercion. Since the state was a coercive institution, it should be secular in the sense that it should not institutionalize, impose or favour a religion, or even support all religions equally. This did not, however, mean that political life should be secular and disallow religiously based appeals, arguments, or actions, as that would violate citizens' religious integrity and their freedom to express their religious identity.

Religions are commonly thought of as closed worlds, almost like sovereign states zealously guarding their territorial boundaries. Their adherents are not allowed to belong to more than one religion or to borrow the ideas and practices of another without feeling guilty or worrying about the dilution of their religious identity. Gandhi took a very different view. For him a religion was not an authoritative, exclusive, and monolithic structure of ideas and practices, but a *resource* from which one freely borrowed whatever one found persuasive. It was thus a collective human property and formed part of mankind's common heritage. Every person was born into and deeply shaped by a particular religious tradition, which as it were constituted his original spiritual home, but other religions were not closed to him. Gandhi said that, as a Hindu, he was an heir to Hinduism's rich and ancient heritage. As an Indian he was a privileged inheritor of India's diverse religious and cultural traditions. As a human being, all great religions were his spiritual inheritance, to which he had as much right as their native adherents. While remaining firmly rooted in his own tradition, he therefore felt free to draw upon their moral and spiritual resources. To express the two central ideas of rootedness and openness, he often used the metaphor of living in a house with its windows wide open. The house was protected by walls and gave him a sense of security and rootedness, but its windows were wide open to allow cultural winds from different directions to blow into it and enrich the air he breathed. 'āno bhadrā kritavo yantu vishvataha' (May noble thoughts from all over the world come to us) was one of his favourite classical maxims.

Gandhi took full advantage of his self-proclaimed intellectual freedom. He abstracted what he took to be the central values of Hinduism and set up a critical dialogue, even a confrontation, between them and those derived from other religious traditions. Thus he took over the concept of *ahimsā* (non-violence) from the Indian traditions, especially the Buddhist and the Jain. However, he found it negative and passive and reinterpreted it in the light of the activist and socially oriented Christian concept of *caritas*. He felt that the latter was too emotive, led to worldly attachments, and compromised the agent's self-sufficiency, and so he redefined it in the light of the Hindu concepts of *anāsakti* (non-attachment) and *nishkām karma* (action without desire). His double conversion, his Christianization of an Indian concept after he had suitably Indianized the Christian concept, yielded the novel idea of an active and positive but detached and non-emotive love. Again, he took over the traditional Hindu practice of fasting as a penance, combined it with the Christian concepts of vicarious atonement and suffering love, interpreted each in the light of the other, and developed the novel idea of 'voluntary crucifixion of the flesh'. It involved fasting undertaken by the acknowledged leader of a community to atone for the evil deeds of his followers, awaken their sense of shame and guilt, and mobilize their moral and spiritual energies for redemptive purposes.

Gandhi's religious eclecticism disturbed many of his Christian and Hindu admirers, who complained that it displayed spiritual shallowness and lack of commitment and did injustice to the traditions involved. His Christian associates argued that, since he had borrowed so much from Christianity, he should take the next logical step of converting to it. For his Hindu followers he should stop 'Christianizing and corrupting' his religion, and stay true to its central values. Gandhi was unrepentant. In his view his so-called eclecticism was really a creative synthesis born out of a sincere and relentless search for Truth, and signified not shallowness but a desire to deepen his own and hopefully other religious traditions and build vitally necessary bridges between them. For him one did not have to be a Christian in order to feel entitled to adopt Christian beliefs and practices. And one who did so did not *become* a Christian. Indeed, the very terms Christian, Hindu, and Muslim were deeply mistaken and a source of much intolerance. They reified the respective religions, set up rigid boundaries between them, sanctioned false proprietary claims, and created a psychological and moral barrier against mutual borrowing.

In the ultimate analysis, argued Gandhi, there were neither Christians nor Hindus, only human beings who freely helped themselves with the moral and spiritual resources of these and other great religious traditions (G 428). One might admire Jesus as a great soul, but also hold the Buddha, Moses, and others in equally high esteem. Those who did so belonged to their particular religions and also to several others. They were Christians, Muslims, or Buddhists in the sense that these religious traditions were their native homes or points of spiritual orientation, and satisfied them the most. However, they also cherished and freely drew upon other religious traditions, and carried parts of these into their own. A sincere spiritual seeker welcomed all valuable insights and grew from 'truth to truth' in his unending journey towards Truth. For Gandhi, to be open to God was to be open to *all* religious traditions. The fundamentalist who attempted to enclose God's infinity within the confines of a single religion and viewed others as rivals or enemies was guilty of moral myopia, spiritual hubris, even blasphemy.

Gandhi's dispute with his critics highlighted two very different approaches to religion and religious truth. For him religion was a resource, a body of insights to be extracted, combined, and interpreted in the way he thought proper. His approach to religion was therefore profoundly ahistorical, uninhibited, anti-traditionalist and liberal, and did not involve understanding religious traditions in their own terms. For his critics a religion was uniquely grounded in a particular historical event, possessed moral and spiritual authority, formed the basis of the relevant community, and required a careful and faithful study of its basic texts. Each approach had its merits and weaknesses. Gandhi's view placed the individual at the centre of the religious search, liberated religion from the stranglehold of traditionalism and literalism, encouraged fresh readings of scriptures, and made space for an inter-religious dialogue. However, it also violated the historical integrity of the religious tradition, de-institutionalized religion, and encouraged in less competent hands an attitude of shallow cosmopolitanism. His critics' approach had the opposite virtues and vices.

Chapter 3
Human nature

Gandhi's theory of human nature was closely bound up with his views on God and religion. It was complex, at places deeply ambiguous, and not entirely consistent. Briefly, and at the risk of some oversimplification, he thought that three fundamental facts characterized human beings. First, they were an integral part of the cosmos. Second, they were necessarily interdependent, and developed and fell together. And third, they were four-dimensional beings made up of the body, the *manas*, the *ātman*, and the *swabhāva*, whose interplay explained their behaviour and formed the basis of morality. We shall take each in turn.

The cosmocentric view

Unlike almost all the major traditions of Western thought, which neatly separate human beings from animals and assign the former a supremely privileged position on earth, Gandhi followed Indian traditions in taking a cosmocentric view of human beings. The cosmos was a well-co-ordinated whole whose various parts were all linked in a system of *yajna*, or interdependence and mutual service. It consisted of different orders of being ranging from the material to the human, each governed by its own laws and standing in a complex relationship with the rest. Human beings were an integral part of the cosmos, and were tied to it by the deepest bonds. In Gandhi's favourite metaphor, the cosmos was not a pyramid of which the material world was the base and human beings the apex, but a series of ever-widening circles encompassing humankind, the sentient world, the material world, and the all-including cosmos. Since the cosmic spirit pervaded or infused the universe and was not outside it, the so-called natural world was not natural or material but spiritual or divine in nature.

Since everything in the universe bore the mark of divinity, it needed to be approached in a spirit of cosmic piety and *maitri* (friendliness). Gandhi thought that the idea that God had given the universe to human beings as a property to be used as they pleased was both incoherent and sacrilegious. The former because God was neither a person nor separate from the universe, the latter because the divine could not be an object of property. The universe was a common inheritance of all living beings, who were equally entitled to its resources and should live in a spirit of mutual accommodation. Being rational, human beings were the custodians of the rest of creation and should respect its rights and cherish its diversity. Since their very existence so required, and since nature constantly reproduced and replenished itself, they might help themselves with such natural resources as they needed to live in moderate comfort. They had no right to take more, for that amounted to 'theft', nor to undermine the regenerative capacity of nature by polluting and poisoning it, by rendering land barren and infertile, or by exhausting its resources.

Since Gandhi considered all life sacred, he vacillated on the question of whether human life was superior to the non-human. By and large he thought that it was, because of the human capacities for rationality and morality. However, the superiority was not 'absolute', for non-human beings too were divine in nature and legitimate members of the cosmos. Human beings might therefore take animal life only when absolutely necessary, and then with a sense of regret. Poisonous snakes and animals, which threatened crops, were not to be killed but caught and released in safe places or driven away. Animals were not to be killed for food except when the climate or local circumstances so required, and never for pleasure or even scientific experiments. The body needed food, which contained life, required the use of insecticides, and involved cultivation with its enormous destruction of life. Gandhi called the body the 'house of slaughter' and was deeply anguished by the violence its survival entailed. Since violence was built into the human condition and thus unavoidable, he thought the only moral course of action was to minimize it by reducing one's wants and to compensate for it by taking tender care of nature.

Human interdependence

That human beings were necessarily interdependent and formed an organic whole was another 'basic' truth about them according to Gandhi. Individuals owed their existence to their parents, without whose countless sacrifices they would neither survive nor grow into sane human beings. They realized their potential in a stable and peaceful society, made possible by the efforts of thousands of anonymous men and women. They became rational, reflective, and moral beings within a rich civilization created by scores of sages, saints, savants, and scientists. In short, every human being owed his humanity to others, and benefited from a world to the creation of which he contributed nothing. For Gandhi human beings were 'born debtors', and involuntarily inherited debts that were too vast to be repaid. Even a whole lifetime was not enough to pay back what they owed their parents, let alone all others. Furthermore their creditors were by their very nature unspecifiable. Most of them were dead or unknown, and those who were alive were so numerous and their contributions so varied and complex that it was impossible to decide what one owed to whom. To talk about 'repaying' the debts did not therefore make sense except as a clumsy and metaphorical way of describing one's response to unsolicited but indispensable gifts.

Given that the debts could never be repaid and the favours returned, all that human beings could do was to 'recognise the conditions of their existence', and continue the ongoing universal system of interdependence by discharging their duties and contributing to collective well-being. They should look upon their lives as *yajna*, an offering at the universal altar, and contribute to the maintenance and enrichment of both the human world and the cosmos. As Gandhi put it, '*Yajna* having come to us with our birth we are debtors all our lives, and thus for ever bound to serve the universe.' Such service was not only their duty but also their right, for without it they lacked the opportunity to fulfil themselves and affirm their dignity. In Gandhi's view, right and duty were inseparable not only in the usual sense that one person's rights created corresponding duties for others, but in the deeper sense that they were two different ways of looking at the same thing. One had a duty to exercise one's rights and a right to discharge one's duties. We shall return to this complex issue later.

Since human beings were necessarily interdependent, every human action was both self- and other-regarding. It affected others and shaped the agent's own character and way of life, and necessarily influenced his relations with others and with himself. When human beings developed themselves, they awakened others to their potentialities and inspired, encouraged, and raised them as well. And when they fell, others too suffered damage. For Gandhi, human beings could not degrade or brutalize others without degrading or brutalizing themselves, or inflict psychic and moral damage on others without inflicting it on themselves as well. This was so in at least three ways. To degrade others was to imply that a human being may be so treated, and thus to lower the moral minimum due to every human being from which all alike suffered. Secondly, to degrade others was to damage their pride, self-respect, and potential for good, and hence both to deny the benefits of their possible contributions and to increase the collective moral, psychological, and financial cost of repairing the damage they were likely to do to themselves and others. Thirdly, as beings capable of morality and critical self-reflection, human beings could not degrade or maltreat others without hardening themselves against the latter's suffering, building up distorted systems of self-justification, coarsening their moral sensibilities, and lowering their own and the collective level of humanity. As Gandhi put it, no man 'takes another down a pit without descending into it himself and sinning in the bargain'. Since humanity was indivisible, every human being was responsible to and for others and should be deeply concerned about how they lived.

Gandhi's concept of indivisible humanity formed the basis of his critique of systems of oppression and exploitation. Such dominant groups as the whites in South Africa, the colonial governments in India and elsewhere, and the rich and the powerful in every society believed that their exploitation and degradation of their respective victims did not in any way damage them as well. In fact it degraded and dehumanized them as much as their victims, and sometimes even more. White South Africans could not deprive blacks of their livelihood and dignity without damaging their own capacity for critical self-reflection and impartial self-assessment, and falling victim to moral conceit, morbid fears, and irrational obsessions. In brutalizing blacks they also brutalized themselves, and were only prevented by their arrogance from noticing how sad and shallow their lives had become. They did enjoy more material comforts, but that made them neither happier nor better human beings. Colonial rulers met the same fate. They could not dismiss their subjects as 'effeminate' and 'childlike' without thinking of themselves as hypermasculine and unemotional adults, a self-image to which they could not conform without distorting and impoverishing their potential. In misrepresenting their subjects, they misrepresented themselves as well and fell into their own traps. They also took home the attitudes, habits, and styles of government acquired abroad, and corrupted their own society. Colonialism did promote their material interests, but only at the expense of their larger and infinitely more important moral and spiritual interests. Since human well-being was indivisible, a system of oppression had no winners, only losers, and it was in the interest of all involved to end it.

Four-dimensionality

In much of Western thought human beings are conceptualized either as bipartite beings made up of the body and the mind or as tripartite beings made up additionally of the soul. In Indian traditions they are theorized differently. Following some of these traditions, Gandhi saw human beings as four-dimensional in nature (M ii. 16–48). They had bodies, which for Gandhi had a twofold ontological significance. The body was self-enclosed, distinct, clearly separated from others, and capable of maintaining its integrity only by preserving its separateness. As such it was the source of the individualist 'illusion' that each human being was self-contained and only externally and contingently related to others. The body was also the seat of the senses, and thus of the wants and desires associated with them. The senses were inherently unruly 'like wild horses' and knew no restraint. Human desires were similar in nature and, being capable of infinite extension, inherently insatiable.

In addition to the body, the human being also had a mind (*manas*). Gandhi's view of the mind was highly complex and somewhat ambiguous. The mind included *chetanā* (stream of consciousness), which began at birth and ended with death. It included *buddhi* (intelligence), which took many forms and operated at several levels, and gave rise to such capacities as discernment, analytical reason, insight, and intuition. The *manas* was also the seat of passions, thoughts, memory, and moods. For Gandhi it was primarily an instrument of knowledge and action, and sought to understand, control, and find its way around in the world. Although distinct from the body, it was closely tied up with it. Reflecting on its worldly experiences as an embodied being, the human mind developed the notion of the ego or self, the source of the human sense of agency and particularity. Since the self desperately strove to preserve its separateness and temporal continuity, the mind was inherently restless and insecure. It was 'crowded' with memories, 'weighed down' by the emotional baggage of the past, obsessed with the future, and lacked suppleness and the capacity for silence.

The *ātman* was the third dimension of human beings. Although it is often translated as soul, and although Gandhi himself sometimes used that term, it is better translated as spirit. As we saw, Gandhi believed that the cosmic spirit permeated or infused all living beings. The *ātman* referred to the cosmic spirit as manifested in them, and represented the divine. For Gandhi, all living beings and not just humans had the *ātman*, it was the same in all of them, and it was not a 'spark' or 'part' of the cosmic spirit as he, borrowing the Christian vocabulary, sometimes remarked, but one with and the same in nature as the totality of the cosmic spirit. As Gandhi put it, 'we have but one soul' and are 'ultimately one'. Since he regarded the heart as the most appropriate metaphor for the soul, he often used the two terms interchangeably.

Being a manifestation of the cosmic spirit, the *ātman* shared many of the latter's basic attributes. Like the cosmic spirit, it was not an entity, a thing or a being, but a 'force', an 'active principle', a 'source of intelligent energy'. It was eternal and indestructible, both active and a spectator, and the ultimate ground of being. The destiny or the inner *telos* of the *ātman* consisted in recognizing its identity with and merging into the cosmic spirit, the state Gandhi called *moksha* or liberation from the illusion of particularity.

Thus far Gandhi's thought was in harmony with the classical Indian traditions, especially the *advaita* or monistic tradition. He now gave it a new twist, and argued that, since the cosmic spirit was manifested in all living, especially human, beings, identification with it consisted in identifying oneself with them in a spirit of universal love and service. By giving the idea of *moksha* such a humanist or worldly orientation and defining spirituality in moral terms, Gandhi gave the Indian traditions an activist turn for which he was both much admired and criticized by his countrymen.

The belief that the *ātman* was not a particle or a spark but the totality of the cosmic spirit led Gandhi, as it had done many a classical Hindu writer, to develop an unusual notion of spiritual power. For him the *ātman* was not a being or a thing but a force, a source of energy. Just as the body was the source of physical energy, the *ātman* was the source of spiritual force or energy. Since the *ātman* was identical with the cosmic spirit, it obviously had access to the latter's infinite energy which, if tapped, could work wonders. Like many an Indian thinker, Gandhi argued that, if the individual were to shed the illusion of particularity or selfhood and become a transparent medium of the cosmic spirit, he would be able to mobilize enormous spiritual energy within himself and exercise great moral and spiritual power over his fellow men. This was for him the secret of the powerful hold of Jesus, Muhammad, and the Buddha over their followers. All through his life Gandhi strove to generate such a spiritual power in himself, which was why his political life was integrally bound up with his pursuit of moral perfection.

Finally, human beings had a distinct *swabhāva* or psychological and moral constitution, made up of various tendencies and dispositions. For Gandhi it was an obvious fact of life that, from their very birth onwards, human beings exhibited different temperaments and psychological and moral inclinations, were drawn to and repelled by different things, and developed according to their inner bent. This unique individual nature was ontologically as important, and as central to their identity, as the universal human nature that they all shared in common. It held the individual together and constituted the ground of his unique being or ontological truth.

The natural uniqueness of each individual needed to be explained. God could not be its source for he loved all human beings equally and would have no obvious reason to endow them differently and unequally. Parents could not be its source either, for their *swabhāva* was often quite different from that of their children. Following almost all the major Indian traditions, Gandhi thought that the only plausible 'hypothesis' was that the individual's *swabhāva* was a product of his previous life. In addition to their physical bodies, human beings possessed a *sukṣma śarira*, a subtle and non-material 'body' or personality. It survived their physical death, persisted through several lives, and formed the basis of their unique personal identity or *swabhāva*. What is mistakenly called transmigration of the 'soul' was really the transmigration of the *sukṣma śarira*. The latter was made up of the 'impressions' or 'traces' left behind by the kind of life lived by the agent in his previous life. Since the subtle or non-material 'body' was the product of the individual's own past deeds, it was capable of alteration in this one, and inclined, but did not determine, him to act in specific ways.

Gandhi also thought that the law of *karma*, like the individual's *swabhāva*, implied rebirth. As we saw, since the cosmic spirit functioned in a rational and orderly manner, not only the natural but also the moral world was subject to unalterable laws. According to such religions as Christianity and Islam, God judges human beings after their death, and sends them to heaven or hell depending on the kind of life they have lived on earth. Like other Indian thinkers Gandhi found this belief incoherent. It presupposed that God was a being or a person, a view he found unacceptable for reasons mentioned earlier. It also implied that the judgement was made after death when human beings could do nothing to mend their ways. For Gandhi, God, or rather the cosmic power, was not a person but Law, and human actions produced their inevitable consequences according to the operations of that Law. Since human beings were responsible for the consequences of their actions and must reap the harvest of all they sowed, and since one life was too short for this, they had to go through several more until they succeeded in securing liberation from the cycle of rebirths.

In Gandhi's view then human beings were four-dimensional in nature, possessing a body, a mind, a non-material personality, and a spirit. The body was acquired at birth and disintegrated at death. The mind derived some of its tendencies from the *swabhāva*, and the rest in the course of life, and was coeval with the body. The *swabhāva*, or subtle non-material personality, though subject to alteration, persisted over several lives and was the seat of intratemporal personal identity. The spirit or soul was eternal and, unlike the other three, identical in all human beings. The body and the soul represented two extreme points of orientation, and the mind was drawn towards both. Whether it more easily followed the demands of the body or the soul depended on the individual's *swabhāva*.

The body was the seat of particularity. It shut up individuals within themselves, reinforced their sense of separateness, and encouraged selfishness. By contrast the soul represented the principle of universality and disposed them to break through the walls of selfhood and become one with all living beings. The body-based illusion of particularity was extremely difficult to shed, and required intense self-discipline, conquest of the senses, sustained self-reflection, meditation, spiritual exercises, and divine grace. Many Indian traditions saw no role for the last but Gandhi did, largely under the *Vaishnavite* influence as mediated by the traditional Christian idea of grace.

Although all human beings had a common spiritual destination, namely *moksha*, they reached it in their own unique manner because of their distinct psychological and spiritual constitution. They had to start by accepting what they were, identify their native dispositions, and progressively move at their own pace and by a path suited to them towards their common destination. The spiritual training, the exercises, the religion, or the way of life that helped some might positively harm others.

The idea of one true religion or path to salvation was therefore logically incoherent. To require all human beings to live by an identical formula was to violate their ontological truth, to treat them as if they were not who they were. Each individual had to discover his own *swabhāva* and follow the spiritual path of development best suited to him. This did not mean that others could not or should not help him. His *swabhāva* was manifest in his behaviour and way of life, and hence his friends, family, and above all a spiritually enlightened guru could feel his spiritual pulse, identify his constitutive tendencies and dispositions, and offer appropriate advice and help. However, it was up to the individual concerned to seek or follow their advice. If he rejected it and made mistakes, he should be left free to do so, not because his life was his or he alone knew his moral interests best as liberals argue, but because he was ontologically unique. Respect for his integrity required that his views and way of life should grow out of *his* way of looking at the world and reflect *his* being or truth. That was why persuasion was qualitatively different from coercion. Unlike the latter, it respected and reinforced the other's wholeness, and ensured that the new way of looking at the world took root in and grew out of his changed being. For Gandhi all compulsion was evil, justified only when an individual's actions had grave social consequences and could not be prevented in any other way. And then no euphemism or verbal sophistry should be allowed to obscure the fact that compulsion violated that individual's truth or integrity and was a regrettable necessity.

Like many Indian philosophers, Gandhi subsumed freedom under truth. Since each individual had his own unique ontological truth or constitution, he needed freedom to discover himself and develop at his own pace. Freedom was the necessary basis and precondition of his ability to be true to himself. To deny a person freedom was to force him to be untrue to himself, to live by someone else's truth, to plant a lie at the very centre of his being. For Gandhi the case for freedom was simple, and the same as that for truthfulness. Respect for truth implied respect for human beings as they were constituted at a given point in time and their need to follow the logic of their being. Love of truth involved love of one's fellow human beings in their uniqueness, not as one would like them to be, and ruled out all attempts to 'force them to be free' or sacrifice them at the altar of an abstract and impersonal ideal.

Moral theory

Gandhi's theory of human nature was the basis of his moral theory. As we saw, morality for him consisted in serving and becoming one with all living beings. Negatively it involved refraining from causing them harm, and positively it involved 'wiping away every tear from every eye' and helping them realize their full moral and spiritual potential. In Gandhi's view, morality and spirituality or religion were inseparable. Since spirituality consisted in becoming one with the cosmic spirit and cultivating the love of all living beings, it necessarily entailed morality. Conversely, the latter was embedded in and presupposed the former. Gandhi's reasoning is not easy to follow. By and large he seems to have thought that, since morality involved unstinting and uncalculating service of all living beings, no human being would have the reason, the disposition, the passion, and the energy to do so without an appropriate spiritual orientation. As he once put it, the moral man was like an honest mercenary, whereas the spiritual man was like an ardent patriot. Both did the right thing, but their actions varied greatly in their flavour, dependability, commitment, and energy.

Although morality required disinterested concern for all living beings, human beings had limited moral capacities, little knowledge of other societies, and limited energy. They should therefore concentrate on those they knew and to whom they were bound by ties of expectations, always making sure that they did not promote their interests at the expense of others. Moral life had to be lived locally and contextually, but the demands of the context had to be constantly judged by the imperatives of universal obligations. For Gandhi this was the only way to guard against both abstract universalism that ignored the demands of those to whom one had special ties and commitments, and an uncritical devotion to the latter in disregard of wider duties.

For Gandhi, service to one's fellow human beings was not a separate and independent activity, but informed all one did. Being a husband, a father, a son, a friend, a neighbour, a colleague, a citizen, an employer, or an employee were not so many discrete roles, each governed by its own distinct norms and values, but different ways of realizing one's humanity and relating to one's fellow men. As a neighbour, for example, one should not only refrain from making a nuisance of oneself but should also help one's neighbours, take an active interest in their well-being and the quality of their surroundings, and help create a vibrant local community. A similar spirit of service and humanity should infuse one's manner of earning one's livelihood, which should be looked upon as a *yajna*, as one's form of participation in the promotion of communal well-being, of which monetary reward was not the purpose but an incidental though necessary consequence. Gandhi thought that, by bringing to his every activity the 'sweet smell of humanity', every person could in his own small way help transform the quality of human relationships and contribute to the creation of a better world. Such a 'quiet, unostentatious service' as consoling a widow, educating a neighbour's child, nursing a sick relative, and shopping for an invalid friend, and thus 'picking up one clod of earth' from the entire mass of human unhappiness, was just as important as the more glamorous forms of social service and political action, and sometimes had more lasting and beneficial results.

Whenever you are in doubt, or when the self becomes too much with you, apply the following test. Recall the face of the poorest and the weakest man whom you have seen, and ask yourself if the step you contemplate is going to be of any use to him. Will he gain anything by it? Will it restore him to a control over his own life and destiny?

Implications

Before concluding this chapter we should note three important features of Gandhi's theory of man. First, it bypassed the traditional Western debate on whether human beings were naturally good or evil. Since human beings had souls and were spiritual in nature, they had a deep *tendency* towards good. However, this did not mean that they always loved and pursued good, for they often lacked true self-knowledge, were subject to the body-based illusion of particularity, and their *swabhāva* might dispose them to do evil. All it meant was that human beings had a deep-seated capacity to perceive and pursue good and would act on it *if* that capacity were to be awakened and activated.

Secondly, Gandhi's theory avoided the familiar homogenizing and monistic impulse inherent in most theories of human nature. For these theories, human beings have a specific nature or essence which dictates how they ought to live. And since the essence is believed to be the same in all, only one way of life is considered to be the best for them and may legitimately be imposed on those falling short of it. Gandhi's view of human nature avoided that danger. Although all human beings had an identical soul or spirit and hence a common destination, they were also naturally unique and had different intermediate goals and ways of realizing them. Gandhi's view thus stressed both human identity and difference, and left ample ontological space for autonomy and diversity. As we saw, he explained human individuality in terms of a dubious theory of rebirth. There is no reason why we cannot reject that theory while appreciating his concern to ground diversity in the very structure of our conception of human nature.

Thirdly, Gandhi was deeply uneasy with the 'European' ideas of rights and duties and their artificial opposition. It is often argued that rights and duties are mutually exclusive in the sense that nothing can be both a right and a duty, and that rights are exercises of, and duties restrictions on, freedom. As we saw, Gandhi viewed the matter very differently. For him the two were as inseparable as two sides of the same coin, and mutually regulative. For example, self-development or personal autonomy was a *right* because each individual was unique and should be free to evolve a way of life suited to his psychological and moral constitution. But it was also a *duty* because that was the only way he could make his distinct contribution to society and discharge his inescapable existential debts. Similarly one had a right to look after one's children because one had brought them into the world and wished to make sure they flourished, as well as a duty because otherwise they would be neglected, not develop into self-determining and morally conscious agents, and become a burden on society. In order to stress the inseparability of rights and duties, Gandhi preferred to use the polysemic Sanskrit term *dharma*, which signified nature, right, and duty. Since every human action was both a right and a duty and had an individual and a social dimension, rights had to be defined and exercised in a socially responsible manner, and duties defined and discharged in a way that took account of the agent's uniqueness and claims (M ii. 65–8; M iii. 496–8).

Chapter 4
Satyāgraha

As someone whose entire life was taken up with fighting against such injustices as racial discrimination in South Africa, British rule in India, and ugly social practices in his own society, Gandhi wondered how a moral person should conduct such struggles. Traditionally people have relied on rational discussion and violence, appealing respectively to reason and the 'body-force'. He found both methods unsatisfactory in varying degrees, and explored one that relied on the hitherto untapped 'soul-force' or 'truth-force'.

The limits of rationality and violence

For Gandhi, rational discussion or persuasion was the best way to resolve conflict. In his view rational discussion worked under two conditions. First, since human beings are fallible and partial, each should make a sincere effort to look at the disputed subject from the other's point of view. If either party were to be dogmatic, self-righteous, or obstinate, it would not be willing to question its view of the matter in dispute, put itself into the shoes of the other, and appreciate why the latter saw things differently.

Secondly, human reason did not operate in a psychological and moral vacuum. Human beings were complex creatures full of prejudices, sympathies, and antipathies, all of which distorted and circumscribed the power of reason. If a person did not care for others, had no fellow-feeling for them, or thought them subhuman, he would not take their interests into account and would find all kinds of reasons to ignore those interests. Even if he rationally appreciated the equal claims of their interests, he would lack the motive to respect and promote them. Gandhi appealed to his own experiences. He had tried to convince white South Africans that blacks and Asians were entitled to equal rights; the British rulers that Indians should be free to govern their own affairs; the high-caste Hindus that untouchability was an abominable practice; and in each case his opponents either failed to see the force of his arguments, or dismissed them by specious counter-arguments, or conceded them but refused or failed to act on them. In Gandhi's view this was because their range of sympathy was too narrow to include their victims. In his favourite language, the head and the heart formed a unity, and if the heart rejected someone, the head tended to do so too. The rationalist belief that human beings were guided and motivated solely by the 'weight' of the argument was false, a 'piece of idolatry', an act of 'blind faith'. Thanks to selfishness, failure of moral imagination, hatred, ill-will, and deep prejudices, human beings did not often have either an open mind or an open heart. Although desirable in principle, rational discussion was of limited value in practice. 'To men steeped in prejudice, an appeal to reason is worse than useless' (iv. 237).

Realizing the limits of rational discussion, many turned to violence as the only effective method of securing justice. Some took a purely instrumental view of it, and thought it fully justified if it produced the desired results. Others agreed it was morally undesirable, but justified it when it was likely to result in the elimination of a greater evil. Gandhi was particularly disturbed by the ease with which violence had been rationalized and used throughout history. He appreciated that it was often born out of frustration, that many who used it hated it and resorted to it only because they saw no other way to fight entrenched injustices, and that much of the blame for its use had to be laid at the doors of morally blind and narrow-minded dominant groups. While he was therefore prepared to condone spontaneous violence under unbearable conditions or grave provocation, he was totally opposed to it as a deliberate method of social change (M ii. 264–87; xxvi. 486–92).

The use of violence denied the ontological facts that all human beings had souls, that they were capable of appreciating and pursuing good, and that no one was so degenerate that he could not be won over by appealing to his fellow-feeling and humanity. Furthermore human beings sincerely disagreed about what was the right thing to do, 'saw truth in fragment and from different angles of vision', and all their beliefs were fallible and corrigible. In Gandhi's view the use of violence denied this. In order to be justified in taking the extreme step of harming or killing someone, one had to assume that one was *absolutely* right, the opponent *totally* wrong, and that violence would *definitely* achieve the desired result. The consequences of violence were irreversible in the sense that a life once terminated or damaged could never be revived or easily put together. And irreversible deeds required infallible knowledge to justify them, which was obviously beyond human reach. Gandhi acknowledged that, taken to its logical extreme, his theory of 'relative truth' undermined the very basis of action, for no man could ever act if he constantly entertained the nagging doubt that he might be wholly mistaken. However, he thought that one should at least acknowledge one's fallibility and leave room for reflection and reconsideration, and that, being irreversible and emotionally charged, violence did not allow this.

Gandhi also rejected violence on moral grounds. Morality consisted in doing what was right because one *believed* it to be right, and required unity of belief and conduct. Since the use of violence did not change the opponent's perception of truth, it compelled him to behave in a manner contrary to his sincerely held beliefs, and violated his moral integrity. Gandhi further argued that violence rarely achieved lasting results. An act of violence was deemed to be successful when it achieved its immediate objectives. However, if it were to be judged by its long-term consequences, our conclusion would have to be very different. Every apparently successful act of violence encouraged the belief that it was the only effective way to achieve the desired goal, and developed the habit of turning to violence every time one ran into opposition. Society thus became used to it and never felt compelled to explore an alternative. Violence also tended to generate an inflationary spiral. Every successful use blunted the community's moral sensibility and raised its threshold of violence, so that over time an increasingly larger amount became necessary to achieve the same results. In Gandhi's view the facts that almost every revolution so far had led to terror, devoured its children, and failed to create a better society were a proof that the traditional theory of revolution was fatally flawed.

Finally, for Gandhi the means–end dichotomy lying at the heart of most theories of violence was false. In human life the so-called means consisted not of implements and inanimate tools but of human actions, and by definition these could not fall outside the jurisdiction of morality. The method of fighting for an objective was not external to but an integral part of it. Every step towards a desired goal shaped its character, and utmost care had to be taken lest it should distort or damage the goal. The goal did not exist *at the end* of a series of actions designed to achieve it; it shadowed them from the very beginning. The so-called means were really the ends in an embryonic form, seeds of which the so-called ends were a natural flowering. Since this was so, the fight for a just society could not be conducted by unjust means.

> A non-violent revolution is not a programme of seizure of power. It is a programme of transformation of relationships, ending in a peaceful transfer of power.

Soul-force

Gandhi concluded that, since the two methods of fighting against
injustice were inadequate or deeply flawed, we needed a new method.
It should activate the soul, mobilize the individual's latent moral
energies, appeal to both the head and the heart, and create a climate
conducive to peaceful resolution of conflict conducted in a spirit of
mutual goodwill. Gandhi thought that his method of *satyāgraha* met
this requirement. He first discovered and tried it out during his
campaigns against racial discrimination in South Africa, and kept
perfecting it in the course of his struggles against British rule in India
and the unjust practices of his own society.

For Gandhi *satyāgraha*, meaning civil insistence on or tenacity in the
pursuit of truth, aimed to penetrate the barriers of prejudice, ill-will,
dogmatism, self-righteousness, and selfishness, and to reach out to and
activate the soul of the opponent. However degenerate or dogmatic a
human being might be, he had a soul, and hence the capacity to feel for
other human beings and acknowledge their common humanity. Even a
Hitler or Mussolini was not beyond redemption. They too loved their
parents, wives, children, friends, and pet animals, thereby displaying the
basic human capacity for fellow-feeling. Their problem was not that
they lacked that capacity but rather that it was limited to a few, and our
task was to find ways of expanding it. *Satyāgraha* was a 'surgery of the
soul', a way of activating 'soul-force'. For Gandhi 'suffering love' was the
best way to do this, and formed the inspiring principle of his new
method. As he put it:

> I have come to this fundamental conclusion that if you want something
> really important to be done, you must not merely satisfy the reason, you
> must move the heart also. The appeal of reason is more to the head, but
> the penetration of the heart comes from suffering. It opens up the inner
> understanding in man. Suffering is the badge of the human race, not the
> sword.   (xlviii. 189)

Confronted with an injustice, the *satyāgrahi* sought a dialogue with his opponent. He did not confront the latter with a dogmatic insistence on the justice of his demands. He knew he could be partial and biased, and invited his opponent to join him in cooperatively searching for the 'truth' or the most just course of action concerning the matter in dispute. As Gandhi put it, 'I am essentially a man of compromise because I am never sure that I am right.' When the dialogue was denied or reduced to an insincere exercise in public relations, the *satyāgrahi* took a principled stand on what he sincerely believed to be his just demands, and patiently and uncomplainingly suffered whatever violence was done to him. His opponent saw him as an enemy or a troublemaker. He refused to reciprocate, and saw him instead as a fellow human being whose temporarily eclipsed sense of humanity it was his duty to restore. Since his sole concern was to evoke a moral response in his opponent, he did everything possible to put him at ease and nothing to harass, embarrass, anger, or frighten him, hoping thereby to trigger in him a slow, intensely personal, and highly complex process of self-examination. The moment his opponent showed willingness to talk in a spirit of genuine goodwill, he suspended the struggle and gave reason a chance to work in a more hospitable climate.

Like Kant and John Rawls, Gandhi argued that every community required a widespread sense of justice to hold it together. But unlike them he argued that the sense of justice was highly cerebral and needed a deeper and emotionally charged sense of shared humanity to give it depth and energy. The sense of humanity consisted in the recognition of the fundamental ontological fact that human well-being was indivisible, that in degrading and brutalizing others human beings degraded and brutalized themselves, and that they could not sustain a shared collective life without a spirit of mutual concern. The sense of humanity constituted the community's vital moral capital, without which it had no defences against or resources to fight the forces of injustice, exploitation, and oppression. The slow and painful task of cultivating and consolidating the sense of humanity, and thereby laying the foundations of a truly moral community, was a collective responsibility, which the *satyāgrahi* took it upon himself to discharge. He assumed the burden of the common evil, sought to liberate both himself and his opponent from its tyrannical automatism, and helped reduce the prevailing level of inhumanity. As Gandhi put it, the old sages 'returned good for evil and killed it'. The *satyāgrahi* took his stand on this 'fundamental moral truth'.

In all his *satyāgrahas* Gandhi observed certain basic principles. They were preceded by a careful study of the situation, patient gathering of facts, a reasoned defence of the objectives, a popular agitation to convince the opponent of the intensity of the *satyāgrahi's* feeling, and an ultimatum to give him a last chance for negotiation. Throughout the *satyāgraha*, the channels of communication with the opponent were kept open, the attitudes on either side were not allowed to harden, and intermediaries were encouraged. The *satyāgrahi* was required to take a pledge not to use violence or to resist arrest or confiscation of his property. Similar rules were laid down for the *satyāgrahi* prisoner, who was expected to be courteous, to ask for no special privileges, to do as he was ordered, and never to agitate for conveniences 'whose deprivation does not involve any injury to his self-respect'.

Gandhi explained the effectiveness of *satyāgraha* in terms of the spiritual impact of suffering love. The *satyāgrahi's love* of his opponent and moral nobility disarmed the latter, defused his feelings of anger and hatred, and mobilized his higher nature. And his uncomplaining *suffering* denied his opponent the pleasure of victory, mobilized neutral public opinion, and created in him a mood conducive to calm introspection. The two together triggered the complex process of critical self-examination on which a *satyāgraha* relied for its ultimate success. Love by itself was not enough, as otherwise the *satyāgrahi* could quietly expostulate with his opponent without launching a campaign, nor was suffering by itself enough, for it had no value and was even counterproductive if accompanied by hatred and anger. Love spiritualized suffering, which in itself had only a psychological value; suffering gave love its psychological energy and moral power. In Gandhi's view, we knew so little about the operations of the human soul that it was not easy to explain rationally how non-violence worked. 'In violence there is nothing invisible. Non-violence, on the other hand, is three-fourths invisible', and it acted in such a 'silent and undemonstrative' manner that its working always retained an air of mystery.

Although Gandhi continued to maintain that suffering love was omnipotent and, when pure, capable of 'melting even the stoniest hearts', he knew that reality was quite different. Most *satyāgrahis* were ordinary human beings whose tolerance, love, determination, and ability to suffer had obvious limits, and their opponents were sometimes too prejudiced and callous to be swayed by their suffering. Not surprisingly, Gandhi was led to introduce such other forms of pressure as economic boycott, non-payment of taxes, non-cooperation, and *hartāl* (cessation of work), none of which relied on the spiritual power of suffering love alone. His vocabulary too became increasingly aggressive. He began to talk of 'non-violent warfare', 'peaceful rebellion', a 'civilized form of warfare', a 'war bereft of every trace of violence', and 'weapons' in the 'armoury' of the *satyāgrahi*, all intended to 'compel' and 'force' the opponent to negotiate. As was to be expected, Gandhi's political realism triumphed over his moral idealism, and, despite his claims to the contrary, his *satyāgrahas* were not always purely spiritual in nature.

In addition to these and other methods, Gandhi introduced the highly controversial method of fasting. He knew that his fasts caused considerable unease among his critics and followers, and went to great lengths to defend them. He argued that his fast was a form of suffering love and had a fourfold purpose. First, it was his way of expressing his deep sense of sorrow and hurt at the way in which those he loved had degraded themselves and disappointed him. Second, as their leader he felt responsible for them, and his fast was his way of atoning for their misdeeds. Third, it was his last desperate attempt, an 'intense spiritual effort', to stir their 'sluggish conscience', to 'sting them into action', and to mobilize their moral energies. For a variety of reasons his countrymen had temporarily lost their senses, as in the case of communal violence, or become insensitive to injustice and suffering, as in the case of untouchability, or had shown utter lack of self-discipline, as when a *satyāgraha* became violent. By suffering himself and inducing sympathetic suffering in them, he said he intended to persuade them to reassess their actions. Finally, the fast was intended to bring the quarrelling parties together and to get them to resolve their differences themselves, thereby both deepening their sense of community and developing their powers of self-determination and conflict-resolution.

Gandhi agreed that his fast exerted considerable pressure on his intended target, but thought it on balance fully justified. Evil had occurred and needed to be fought. Moral appeals had failed. He could therefore either acquiesce in the evil, which was immoral, or use the only means available to a man of non-violence. The fast did exert moral pressure, but there was nothing improper in it. And it was not coercion or blackmail because it did not threaten others with personal harm. Obviously they did not want him to die, but that was because they loved him, and there was nothing immoral in appealing to their love in this way, especially when its purpose was to make them better human beings.

Since the fast could easily be misused for selfish purposes and even degenerate into blackmail, Gandhi imposed strict limits on it. First, it could only be undertaken against those with whom one was bound by the ties of love and never against strangers, which was why his fasts were directed against his countrymen and rarely against the colonial government. Secondly, the fast must have a concrete and clearly specified purpose, which its addressee can easily understand and respond to. Thirdly, the purpose must be morally defensible especially in the eyes of its intended target. Fourthly, it should not in any way be designed to serve one's personal interests. Fifthly, it should not ask people to do what they are incapable of doing, or involve great sacrifices. And finally, it should only be undertaken by one who is an acknowledged moral leader of his people, has a long record of working for their welfare, and an unblemished moral character (xxiv. 95–9; xxv. 199–202).

The limits of *satyāgraha*

Gandhi's theory of *satyāgraha*, which goes right to the heart of his theory of human nature, was a highly original and creative contribution to theories of social change and political action. He was right to stress the limits of rational discussion and the dangers of violence, and explore new forms of political praxis that broke through the narrow straitjacket of the reason–violence dichotomy. *Satyāgraha* took full account of the rational and moral nature of human beings and stressed the value of rational discussion and moral persuasion. And it was also sensitive to the human capacities for intransigence and moral blindness and sought to overcome these by awakening the shared humanity of the parties involved and transforming their mutual perceptions and relationships. *Satyāgraha* aimed not just to resolve existing disagreements but to build deeper moral and emotional bonds, and thus both give the compromise reached a firmer foundation and make future conflicts less likely and less intractable.

While the moral and political significance of Gandhi's *satyāgraha* is beyond doubt, it is not the panacea he thought it was. Although he was right to stress the unity of reason and morality, or the head and the heart as he called it, he was wrong to think that all or even most social conflicts could be resolved by touching the opponent's heart. They sometimes occur because persons of goodwill take very different views of what constitutes human well-being. On the basis of the principle of the sanctity of human life, some find abortion, euthanasia, and war morally unacceptable while others reach the opposite conclusion. It is difficult to see how Gandhi's method can resolve these differences and the consequent conflicts.

Gandhi was probably right to argue that human beings are generally affected by the suffering of others and regret that suffering even if they are unable or unwilling to do anything about it. However, he overlooked the fact that, if they thought the suffering deserved, their reaction would be different. Not the suffering *per se* but one's judgement of it determines one's response to it, and that in turn depends on one's beliefs about which individuals may deeply disagree. The Sharpeville massacre left many a white South African unmoved, the pictures of the Vietnamese victims of American napalm bombs did not disturb the consciences of many Americans, and the brutal Nazi treatment of the Jews had no effect on many a German.

Gandhi was wrong to argue that *satyāgraha* never failed and that it was effective under all conditions. If he had said that it was a self-chosen way of being in the world and that one would die rather than kill irrespective of the outcome, his view would have made moral though not political sense. To his credit he insisted that *satyāgraha* was meant to succeed and achieve practical results. And that subjected his claim to a different kind of scrutiny. It was an article of faith for him that all human beings had souls, which could be 'touched' and 'activated'. As a result he did not and could not acknowledge that some human beings might be profoundly distorted and beyond hope. *Satyāgraha* presupposes a sense of decency on the part of the opponent, an open society in which his brutality can be exposed, and a neutral body of opinion that can be mobilized against him. It also presupposes that the parties involved are interdependent, as otherwise non-cooperation by the victims cannot affect the vital interests of their opponents, and that the victims have both sufficient self-confidence and a reasonably effective organization to fight against injustices. Human skeletons in the Nazi concentration camps could hardly have launched a *satyāgraha*, nor would it have succeeded in a closed and ruthless totalitarian system. As Martin Buber wrote to Gandhi, where there is no witness, there can be no martyrdom, and without the latter *satyāgraha* loses its moral force. Hayim Greenberg, editor of *The Jewish Frontier* and an admirer of Gandhi, wrote to him, 'a Jewish Gandhi in Germany, should one arise, could function for about five minutes and would be promptly taken to the guillotine'. Gandhi replied that Hitler too was a human being, that the Jews, who were going to be slaughtered anyway, should have asserted their dignity and freely chosen their way of death, and that such an action was bound to have an effect on ordinary Germans, if not immediately at least a little later (lxviii. 137–41). His reply had a point, but it rested on an uncritical faith in the power of non-violence, and showed little understanding of the complex ways in which totalitarian systems brutalized the community, demoralized the victims, distorted public discourse, and undermined the basic preconditions of *satyāgraha*.

Gandhi's *satyāgraha* has much to be said for it, but it cannot be a catholicon. Although Gandhi insisted otherwise, violence need not be accompanied by hatred and ill-will or be uncontrolled. Like non-violence it too can be restrained, measured, born out of love for both the victims and the perpetrators of injustice, and used to arrest human degradation. Gandhi would have been wiser to insist not on one 'sovereign' method of action but on a plurality of methods to be used singly or in combination with others as the situation required. Since different circumstances require different responses, violence might sometimes achieve results that non-violence either cannot or do so only at an unacceptably high price in human suffering.

Although Gandhi's *satyāgraha* had its limitations and he was wrong to claim 'sovereign efficacy' for it, it is a powerful, novel, and predominantly moral method of social change. Not surprisingly, it has been borrowed and tried out in different countries with suitable adjustments to local circumstances. The United States is an excellent example of this. Many black American leaders had gone to India from the early 1930s onwards to seek his advice and study his method. He was so impressed with their commitment that he remarked that 'it may be through the Negroes that the unadulterated message of non-violence will be delivered to the world' (ixii. 202). The American civil rights movement of the 1950s and 1960s under the leadership of Martin Luther King confirmed Gandhi's hope. Embarking on 'a serious intellectual quest for a method to eliminate social evil', King turned to a number of writers including Marx, and found them all unhelpful. A sermon by Mordecai Johnson, the then President of Howard University, in 1950 alerted him to the importance of Gandhi's *satyāgraha*. King read Gandhi closely, found 'intellectual and moral satisfaction' in his writings, and wrote (K 73):

> As I read I became deeply fascinated by [Gandhi's] campaigns of non-violent resistance ... The whole concept of '*Satyāgraha*' ... was profoundly significant to me. As I delved deeper into the philosophy of Gandhi my scepticism concerning the power of love gradually diminished, and I came to see for the first time its potency in the area of social reform. Prior to reading Gandhi, I had about concluded that the ethics of Jesus were only effective in individual relationships ... But after reading Gandhi, I saw how utterly mistaken I was. Gandhi was probably the first person in history to lift the love ethic of Jesus above mere interaction between individuals to a powerful and effective social force on a large scale ... It was in this Gandhian emphasis on love and non-violence that I discovered the method for social reform that I had been seeking for so many months.

King shared Gandhi's belief in the power of suffering love, his abhorrence of violence, emphasis on both the head and the heart, concern to raise the consciousness and build up the self-confidence of the victims of injustice, and stress on the crucial role of effective organization and an inspiring leader. King, however, could not apply Gandhi's method to the American situation without suitably revising it.

He was a Christian, and hence Gandhi's metaphysics had only a limited appeal to him. As he put it, 'Christ furnished the spirit and motivation [for non-violent resistance], while Gandhi furnished the method' (K 67). Gandhi's fasts, his belief in the spiritual power of personal purity, and the concomitant emphasis on simple living and the conquest of the senses had no attraction for King. This is puzzling for Christ's crucifixion is the central motif of Christianity, and one would have expected King to explore ways of reaffirming and re-enacting it and mobilizing its immense symbolic potential in his repertoire of political action, as Gandhi did with his fasts. Again, given the fact that King was operating within a largely democratic context and wanted black integration into American society, Gandhi's method of non-cooperation with the established legal, political, and cultural institutions was of little relevance to him. In some respects King seems to have been more acutely aware than Gandhi of the power of evil (an awareness reinforced by the intellectual influence of the American Protestant theologian Reinhold Niebuhr, who both admired and stressed the limits of Gandhi's non-violence), and guarded himself and his followers against the 'illusions of a superficial optimism concerning human nature and the dangers of a false idealism' (K 81). King's civil rights movement showed both the universal relevance of Gandhi's *satyāgraha* and the need for its creative adaptation and development.

Chapter 5
Critique of modernity

Modern industrial civilization has been a subject of much agonized debate since its emergence in the early years of the nineteenth century. It is characterized by such features as rationalism, secularization, industrialization, the scientific culture, individualism, technological mastery of nature, the drive towards globalization, and liberal democracy. Few writers were entirely happy or unhappy with all of these. The only question was whether they thought that on balance modern civilization was a force for good or evil. The answer depended on their criteria of evaluation, the way in which they related its desirable and undesirable features, and whether in their view the latter were contingent and eliminable or deeply embedded in and hence inseparable from its overall structure. Not surprisingly such writers as J. S. Mill, Alexis de Tocqueville, Thomas Carlyle, Thoreau, Ruskin, Tolstoy, Marx, Max Weber, and Emile Durkheim reached different conclusions. Whether they admired, criticized, or condemned modernity, they all did so from a European perspective.

Lack of self-restraint

Although Gandhi had the advantage of observing modern civilization from both the European and non-European perspectives, he was more familiar with and sympathetic to the latter, and saw it primarily through the eyes of one of its victims. He called it modern rather than European or Western partly to highlight its historical specificity, and partly to emphasize that Europe itself had long nurtured a different civilization that had much in common with its non-European counterparts, including the Indian.

For Gandhi, every civilization was inspired and energized by a distinct conception of human beings. If that conception was mistaken, it corrupted the entire civilization and made it a force for evil. In his view that was the case with modern civilization. Although it had many achievements to its credit, it was fundamentally flawed, as was evident in the fact that it was aggressive, imperialist, violent, exploitative, brutal, unhappy, restless, and devoid of a sense of direction and purpose. Gandhi thought that this was because modern civilization neglected the soul, privileged the body, misunderstood the nature and limits of reason, and had no appreciation of the individual *swabhāva*. In the light of our earlier discussion, it is easy to see why Gandhi thought that such a view radically misconceived and violated the inner balance and hierarchy of human nature (M i. 199–264).

As we saw, the body had two basic characteristics for Gandhi. It enclosed the agent within himself or herself and bred individualism, and it was the seat of desires. Since modern civilization privileged the body, it was necessarily driven by the two interdependent principles of self-interest and undisciplined self-indulgence. It was appetitive, dominated by desires, given over to unrestrained satisfaction of wants, and lacked a sense of limits and moral depth. It was 'materialist' in its nature and orientation in the sense that it valued material possessions and consumption to the exclusion of almost everything else, and made the economy its centre. Driven by greed and ruthless competition, the economy led to the accumulation of vast amounts of wealth in the hands of a 'few capitalist owners'. They had only one aim, to make profit, and only one means to do so, to produce goods that satisfied people's ever-increasing wants. They had a vital vested interest in constantly whetting jaded appetites, planting new wants, and creating a mental climate in which not to want the goods daily pumped into the market was to be abnormal. Not surprisingly, little value was attached to self-discipline or moral regulation of desires, the very emblem of human dignity.

> Civilization, in the real sense of the term, consists not in the multiplication but in the deliberate and voluntary restriction of wants. This alone promotes real happiness and contentment and increases the capacity for service.

The capitalist search for profits led to mechanization and 'industrialism'. In Gandhi's view, machines relieved drudgery, created leisure, increased efficiency, and were indispensable when there was a shortage of labour. Their use should be guided by a well-considered moral theory indicating how human beings should live, spend their free time, and relate to one another. Since modern civilization lacked such a theory and was only propelled by the search for profit, it mechanized production without any regard for the wider moral, cultural, and other consequences. Machines were introduced when there was no obvious need for them and even when they were likely to throw thousands out of work. For Gandhi, mechanization or the fetishism of technology was closely tied up with the larger phenomenon of industrialism, another apparently self-propelling and endless process of creating larger and larger industries with no other purpose than to produce cheap consumer goods and maximize profit. Since modern economic life followed an inexorable momentum of its own without anyone being in charge of it, it reduced human beings to helpless and passive spectators and represented a new form of slavery, more comfortable and invidious and hence more dangerous than the earlier ones.

Based on the beliefs that unless one was constantly on the move one was not alive, and that the faster the tempo of life the more alive one was, modern civilization was inherently restless and lacked stability. It aimed to conquer time and space and developed increasingly speedier modes of transport and communication. Cars were replaced by trains, and the latter by planes, but no one asked why one needed to travel so fast and what one intended to do with the time saved. Thanks to its restlessness and 'mindless activism', mistakenly equated with dynamism and energy, modern civilization undermined man's unity with his environment and fellow men, and destroyed stable and long-established communities. In the absence of natural and social roots and the stable and enduring landmarks which alone gave human beings a sense of identity and continuity, they had become abstract, indeterminate, empty, and related to each other at best by mutual indifference, at worst by mutual hostility.

As a result moral life suffered a profound distortion. It became as abstract as the human beings whose relations it regulated, and replaced virtues by a set of impersonal rules. Morality was seen not as an expression and realization of human dignity, but as a restriction of freedom, a kind of tax one had to pay in order to be able to enjoy one's residual freedom unhindered. It was therefore reduced to the barest minimum, requiring little more than what was needed to prevent people from harming or destroying each other.

Since moral life lacked the nourishing soil of the sentiments of goodwill and mutual concern, it increasingly depended on the non-moral motive of fear. Modern man took care not to harm others lest they should harm him, and he did a good turn to them as an investment for the future. Morality was reduced to reciprocal egoism or enlightened self-interest. Since self-interest was not a moral principle, Gandhi argued that enlightened self-interest was not one either. In modern civilization, morality was a form of prudence, a more effective way of pursuing self-interest, and was virtually exorcized out of existence.

In Gandhi's view, modern civilization denuded morality of its vital internal dimension and ignored what he called the quality of the soul. For him jealousy, hatred, meanness, ill-will, perverse pleasure at another's misfortunes, and sordid thoughts and fantasies were moral impurities reflecting an ill-developed and coarse soul, and the moral agent should endeavour to eliminate them. Being concerned only to get on in the world and lead a comfortable life, modern man not only saw no value in the purity of his soul and the quality of his motives but also found such preoccupations a hindrance. Not a generous, reflective, self-critical, sensitive, and tender-hearted but a tough, aggressive, ambitious, and self-centred person was the ideal and the necessary basis of modern civilization.

Modern man, Gandhi went on, spent most of his energy trying to steady himself in a hostile and unstable environment. He had neither the inclination nor the ability to slow down the tempo of his life, be alone with himself, look inwards, reflect on his pattern of life, and nurture the inner springs of energy. He lived outside himself and was exhausted both physically and spiritually. Inwardly empty and frightened to face himself, he was easily bored, and feverishly looked for new sources of energy and amusement. Gandhi thought that modern civilization had a depressing air of 'futility' and 'madness' about it and was likely to destroy itself before long.

In Gandhi's view the exploitation of one's fellow human beings was built into the very structure of modern civilization. Consumers were constantly manipulated into desiring things they did not need and which were not in their long-term interest. Workers were made to do boring jobs at subsistence wages under inhuman conditions, and given little opportunity or encouragement to develop their intellectual and moral potential. The poor were treated with contempt, weaker races were regarded as subhuman and bought and sold, and weaker nations were conquered and mercilessly oppressed and exploited. For Gandhi European imperialism was a natural expression of the aggressive and exploitative impulse lying at the heart of modern civilization.

In Gandhi's view modern civilization rested on and was sustained by massive violence. It involved violence against oneself for, in a society of ambitious, competitive, and mutually fearful persons, no one could flourish or even survive without developing a regimented and aggressive psyche. It also involved violence against other persons at both the personal and collective levels. Since individuals felt threatened by others and desperately sought to keep them at a manageable distance, they relied on the use or threat of verbal, emotional, moral, and even physical violence, ultimately backed up by the concentrated violence of the state. Relations between organized groups, classes, and states were even more tense and aggressive and scarred by open or cold wars. Modern civilization also involved an egregious amount of violence against nature. The latter's resources were ruthlessly exploited and its rhythm and balance disturbed, and the animals were freely killed or tortured for food, sport, fancy clothes, and medical experiments. In Gandhi's view violence 'oozed from every pore' of modern society, and had so much become a way of life that human beings today were in danger of losing the capacity to notice its pervasive presence, let alone find ways of dealing with it. Although it claimed to be based on such values as human dignity, equality, freedom, and civility, modern civilization was inherently militarist and violent. The colonial conquests, slavery, the two world wars, the countless civil and external wars that had characterized European history for the past few centuries, the Nazi murder of Jews, and so on formed a pattern too consistent and recurrent to be dismissed as accidents or aberrations. When once asked what he thought of European civilization, Gandhi replied that 'it would be a good idea'.

Naive rationalism

For Gandhi another great weakness of modern civilization was its failure to understand the nature and limits of reason. It defined reason in largely positivist terms, made it the sole source of knowledge and action, and indiscriminately extended it to all areas of life. In other words it made a 'fetish' of reason and constructed an untenable and ultimately 'irrational' ideology of rationalism. Gandhi saw reason as an important human faculty with an indispensable role in human life, but rationalism was an altogether different matter. As he put it:

> Every formula of every religion has in this age of reason to submit to the test of reason and universal assent ... But rationalism is a hideous monster when it claims for itself omnipotence. Attribution of omnipotence to reason is as bad a piece of idolatry as is worship of stock and stone believing it to be God. I plead not for the suppression of reason, but an appreciation of its inherent limits.

Gandhi believed that rationalism was a false and pernicious doctrine. Certain areas of human experience such as religion transcended reason and required faith. They obviously had to satisfy reason but they could not be confined within its narrow limits. In addition, in some areas of human experience such as morality and politics, reason was inherently inadequate and needed to be guided by wisdom, tradition, conscience, intuition, and moral insight. Since the conclusions of reason were necessarily tentative and liable to constant subversion by superior arguments, they could never form the basis of human life. Rationalism valued only one form of knowledge, namely the scientific. It therefore marginalized, ignored, or suppressed many valuable human faculties and forms of knowledge and had a deep anti-pluralist bias and a strong streak of intolerance. According to it human life was transparent, fully knowable if not today then tomorrow, and whatever could not be scientifically known either did not exist or was not worth knowing. Rationalism therefore bred the 'arrogant' and 'irrational' belief that human beings had the ability to shape the world in the way they liked. It lacked a sense of its own limits, a feel for the contingency and unpredictability of life, a capacity to listen to the half-articulated whispers of the human soul and to live with ambiguities.

Rationalism also abstracted reason from other human faculties and the wider way of life, and used it to judge and grade individuals and societies and to justify the domination of those deemed to be less rational. For Gandhi rationalism was inherently hierarchical and missionary, and had a deep imperialist orientation. He had in mind the ways in which racists in South Africa and British imperialists in India treated their subjects and legitimized their rule. Finally, rationalism had a tendency to homogenize individuals and suppress their diversity. It set up identical ideals for all human beings, held up only one kind of life as the highest or truly human, and expected all to conform to it. It thus ignored both their inescapably unique *swabhāva* and the vastly different ways in which they defined and led the good life. Gandhi thought that each individual had his own distinct identity, and was rooted in a specific cultural tradition. What was good for others was not necessarily good for him, and even when it was, he had to achieve it in his own unique way. Rationalism ignored this vital truth and violated human integrity.

Statist culture

Gandhi argued that the highly centralized and bureaucratic modern state enjoying and jealously guarding its monopoly of political power was a necessary product of modern civilization. Competitive and aggressive persons ruthlessly pursuing their interests could only be held together by an intimidating and well-armed state. Since they were strangers to one another and lacked the bonds of goodwill and mutual concern, their relations could only be regulated by impersonal rules enforced by a powerful and bureaucratic state capable of reaching out to all areas of individual life. The centralization of production in the modern economy created social and economic problems of national and international magnitude, and again required a centralized political agency to deal with them. Unemployment, poverty, and the social and economic inequalities created by the modern economy led to acute and legitimate discontent, and required a well-armed state to deter desperate citizens from resorting to violence. The centralized modern state was also necessary to protect international markets and overseas investments.

For Gandhi the state had a vested institutional interest in remaining at the centre of social life and creating the illusion that the problems of society were too complex and intractable to be solved by ordinary citizens acting individually or collectively, and were best left to the state and its official agencies. Even as the state monopolized all political initiative and fostered a statist political culture, it tended to monopolize all morality. Since its isolated and morally impoverished citizens lacked organic bonds and the capacity to organize and run their social relations themselves, the state was the sole source of moral order. The state came to be seen as the highest moral institution whose preservation was a supreme moral value justifying often pointless sacrifices of human lives. All moral sentiments were sucked into it, all moral energies were appropriated by it, all moral norms were judged in terms of its interests, and its laws were deemed to be the sole determinants of collective morality. Dying for the state was considered a supreme virtue, and fighting in its wars the highest duty. Disobeying its laws was strongly disapproved of, and all attempts to weigh its actions in the moral scale were discouraged, on the ground that political life was either inherently amoral or governed by its own distinct morality.

Almost like Marx, Gandhi argued that, although the state claimed to be a moral institution transcending narrow group interests and pursuing the well-being of the whole community, it was in fact little more than an arena of conflict between organized interests, manipulated and controlled by the more powerful among them. Since persons of independent spirit and honour generally avoided it, it was largely in the care of morally shallow individuals keen to forge convenient alliances with and pursuing the interests of dominant groups. Gandhi thought that in these respects the democratic government was no better than the undemocratic, being just as vulnerable to the pressures of the dominant classes and just as ruthless and ready to use violence to protect their interests. Whatever the rhetoric, modern democracy was basically a form of government in which a 'few men capture power in the name of the people and abuse it', a 'game of chess' between rival parties with the people as 'pawns'. Although the fact that a democratic government was periodically elected by and accountable to ordinary people made a difference, it also served to 'camouflage' and confer moral legitimacy on class rule. Gandhi took a dim view of parliamentary democracy. It was in the grip of the dominant party, was not subject to regular popular control, and its debates often bore little relevance to issues of long-term interest to citizens.

> I look upon an increase of the power of the state with the greatest fear, because while apparently doing good by minimizing exploitation, it does the greatest harm to mankind by destroying individuality, which lies at the root of all progress.

Response to modernity

Although Gandhi was convinced that the foundations of modern civilization were 'rotten', he did not dismiss it altogether and praised what he took to be its three great achievements. First, he admired its scientific spirit of inquiry. He observed:

> I have been a sympathetic student of the Western social order, and I have discovered that underlying the fever that fills the soul of the West, there is a restless search for Truth. I value that spirit. Let us study our Eastern institutions in that spirit of scientific inquiry.

(xxxii. 219)

Not that the scientific spirit was unknown in the pre-modern West or ancient India. Rather it was stifled by traditionalists and denied the full scope it had received in the modern age. For Gandhi the scientific spirit stood for intellectual curiosity, rigorous pursuit of truth, and critical examination of established beliefs. While modern civilization was right to cherish it, it defined this spirit in narrowly positivist and aggressive terms and extended it to areas of life where it was least applicable. Here as elsewhere it grasped an important truth but turned it into a falsehood by misunderstanding it and ignoring its limits.

For Gandhi the second great achievement of modern civilization consisted in understanding the natural world and bringing it under greater human control. Being body-centred, it concentrated most of its energies on improving the material conditions of life. It had developed the human capacity to anticipate and control natural calamities, eliminate diseases, improve health and public hygiene, prolong life, and reduce or relieve human drudgery. Gandhi contended that since these and other achievements were secured within a fundamentally flawed framework, they had suffered a profound distortion. It was important to preserve and prolong life, but modern civilization had turned it into the highest value and cultivated a morbid fear of death. Machines had a place in life, but modern civilization had no theory of how to use them and within what limits.

Third, in Gandhi's view modern civilization had greatly contributed to the organizational side of life. It cultivated civic virtues, respect for rules, the capacity to subordinate the personal to collective interest, public morality, mutual respect, and punctuality. Gandhi argued that, although he had 'thankfully copied' many of these 'great' qualities without which his personal and especially political life would have been poorer, modern civilization had once again misinterpreted them and ignored their limits. It reduced morality to enlightened self-interest and undermined its autonomy. It rightly subordinated the individual to collective interest, but failed to provide sufficient room for diversity. It rightly stressed the value of organization, but over-institutionalized human life and left no space for conscientious objection and the lonely dissenter. It was right to emphasize rules, but wrong not to appreciate that they could never exhaust moral life and were precarious unless grounded in finer human impulses.

For Gandhi, then, modern civilization was a highly complex human achievement, and the response to it had to be equally complex, avoiding both its uncritical glorification and undiscriminating rejection. The foundations of modernity were shaky but it had genuine achievements to its credit. Since the latter were secured within a fundamentally mistaken framework, they had to be purged of their distortions before they could be incorporated into a more satisfactory framework. For example, it was not enough to say that mechanization was bad but the machines were good, or that rationalism should be rejected but the spirit of rational inquiry retained. Modern machines were products of the materialist civilization which determined their nature, place in life, and mode of operation, and were not culturally neutral. A differently constituted civilization had to use the available scientific knowledge to develop different kinds of machines and put them to different uses. Other achievements of modern civilization had to be subjected to a similar critical and 'cleansing' process.

An assessment

Although Gandhi's citique of modern civilization bore a strong resemblance to those of Rousseau, Ruskin, Tolstoy, and Marx, it contained several original insights derived from the two great advantages he enjoyed over them. As one belonging to a despised race and an oppressed country, he grasped the darker side of modern civilization with unusual clarity. He saw that although Europe championed the great ideals of human dignity, freedom, and equality, it defined them in an ideologically biased manner and used them to justify slavery, colonialism, racism, and other patently evil practices.

Furthermore, as an heir to the rich and differently structured Indian civilization, Gandhi brought to his critique of modern civilization a perspective not easily available to its Western critics. He was able to see it from the outside and uncover its hidden assumptions, contradictions, and limitations. He saw that contrary to its self-understanding, modern civilization was suffused with the spirit of aggression and violence, that its conception of rationality was narrow and biased, that its view of morality was impoverished and shallow, that its approach to religion was excessively credal and dogmatic, and that its view of individual and collective identity ignored their inherently porous, fluid, and ambiguous nature.

Gandhi's advantages were also his disadvantages. Since he largely concentrated on the darker side of modern civilization, he overlooked some of its great achievements and strengths. And since he saw it from the outside, he oversimplified it and failed to appreciate its complex structure and the full range and depth of its moral vision. Although preoccupied with the endless satisfaction of material desires, modern civilization is also guided by the search for personal independence and autonomy, a non-hierarchical social structure, social justice, and the passionate concern to understand the human world and master the natural environment. It encourages selfishness and greed, but it also fosters human unity, individuality, equality, liberty, creativity, rationality, intellectual curiosity, and all-round human development. And although it conveniently misdefines some of these values and restricts them to the privileged few, that neither diminishes their world-historical importance nor detracts from the fact that they represent a collective human heritage. Materialist at one level, modern civilization also has a moral and spiritual dimension.

Gandhi's analysis of modern civilization made it difficult for him to give an adequate account of what he took to be its major achievements. He treated the rise of the scientific spirit and the development of the civil and organizational virtues as if they were accidental products of modern civilization, and failed to appreciate that they were deeply bound up with it and could not have developed outside it. Gandhi was thus caught up in the paradoxical position of wanting to appropriate part of the 'spirit' of modern civilization while rejecting the very institutions and social structure that embodied and nurtured it. This does not mean that one must accept or reject modern civilization *in toto*, but rather that one needs to take a more dialectical view of it than Gandhi did, showing the internal relations between its strengths and limitations and using its own emancipatory potentialities to go beyond it.

Chapter 6
The vision of a non-violent society

Deeply unhappy with the basic thrust of modern civilization, Gandhi spent most of his adult life exploring an alternative. In Western thought such exploration has generally taken the form of constructing a utopian or ideal society. Gandhi believed that, since different societies had different histories and traditions, the search for a single model was both incoherent and dangerous. It reproduced and reinforced the positivist rationalism of modern society, and encouraged the tendency to shape all societies in a single mould. For him, all that a critic could and should do was to suggest the general principles that should govern the good society, leaving each society free to realize them in its own unique way.

Gandhi's regulative principles of the good society were derived from his theory of human nature discussed earlier. As we saw, human beings were for him the trustees of the rest of creation, interdependent, and four-dimensional in nature. In Gandhi's view these ontological 'truths' yielded the following principles. First, the good society should be informed by the spirit of cosmic piety. Since human beings were not masters or owners but guardians of the rest of creation, they should so organize their collective life that it respected the latter's integrity, diversity, rhythm, and inner balance, and made no more demands on it than was required by a life of moderate comfort.

Secondly, since human beings are interdependent, the good society should discourage all forms of exploitation, domination, injustice, and inequality, which necessarily coarsen human sensibilities and depend on falsehoods for their continued existence, and should find ways of institutionalizing and nurturing the spirit of love, truthfulness, social service, cooperation, and solidarity.

Thirdly, since human beings are spiritual in nature, the good society should help them develop their moral and spiritual powers and create the conditions for *swarāj* (self-rule or autonomy). For Gandhi *swarāj* referred to a state of affairs in which individuals were morally in control of themselves, did what was right, resolved their differences and conflicts themselves, and dispensed with external coercion. They possessed an uncompromising sense of independence and self-respect, and found it a matter of shame to turn to the state or any other external agency to discipline them and regulate their social relations. For Gandhi *swarāj* thus presupposed self-discipline, self-restraint, a sense of mutual responsibility, the disposition neither to dominate nor be dominated by others, and a sense of *dharma*. A free society could not be sustained in the absence of these and related moral powers and virtues. Without them individual liberty was liable to constant misuse, produced consequences harmful to the moral agent as well as others, required an increasingly powerful state to deal with these consequences, and thus ultimately negated itself. Gandhi thought this to be the case with the liberal society of the West, whose much-vaunted liberty never amounted to genuine *swarāj* or self-rule.

Fourthly, the good society should cherish epistemological pluralism. It should appreciate that reason, intuition, faith, traditions, intergenerationally accumulated collective wisdom, and emotions are all valuable sources of knowledge, and make their own distinct contributions to understanding and coping with the complexities of human life. The good society should encourage a dialogue, a creative interplay, between them, and not allow one of them to acquire a hegemonic role or become the arbiter of all others. For Gandhi reason was an important human faculty and all claims to knowledge should pass its test, but that did not mean other human faculties should mimic it or function and validate their claims to knowledge in the same way as it did.

Finally, since each individual has a distinct *swabhāva* or moral and psychological constitution and comes to terms with life in his or her own unique way, the good society should provide the maximum space for personal autonomy. It should respect each person's 'truth' or integrity and allow them the freedom to plan their lives. They might make mistakes, but should be left free to learn from them. Since human lives overlap and since each human being is his brother's keeper, they have a duty to point out each other's limitations in a spirit of charity and love and render such help as is needed. However, this should not involve any form of coercion, least of all the legal, except when their behaviour damages clearly defined collective interests.

Gandhi applied these principles to different areas of life, especially the economic and the political. We shall take each in turn. He frequently observed that his guiding principles were far more important than his specific proposals, and that those who shared the former might legitimately disagree with the latter. His proposals, furthermore, were made in the Indian context and, unlike his guiding principles, did not claim universal applicability.

The economy

For Gandhi both capitalism and communism, the two dominant economic systems of his time, were morally unacceptable. Capitalism was based on the morally problematic institution of private property. Since human powers and talents were socially derived, they were a social trust and could not form the basis of private property. Nature too was a collective human heritage, and could not be privately owned. And since every manmade object was a product of social cooperation, no single individual had an exclusive claim on it. Furthermore capitalism was driven by greed, encouraged aggressive competitiveness, multiplied wants, ruthlessly exploited nature, created vast inequalities, fostered arrogance among the rich and a deep sense of inferiority and hatred among the poor, and in general degraded all (M iii. 467–78).

Although communism was free of some of these evils, it had others, and was just as bad, if not worse. It was materialist and consumerist in its orientation and did not represent a higher civilization. Although it encouraged sharing and cooperation, it imposed these by force and did little to develop the moral energies of its citizens. It insisted on uniformity and ignored the demands of individual *swabhāva*. Since it invested the state with both economic and political power, its statism posed the gravest threat to human dignity and self-respect. Above all, communism was established and continued by means of massive violence with all its attendant evils (M iii. 552–95).

As an alternative to both, Gandhi proposed his well-known theory of trusteeship. It was intended to avoid the evils and combine the advantages of the capitalist and communist forms of ownership, and represented an attempt to socialize property without nationalizing it. A rich man was allowed to retain his property, but was expected to hold his wealth and personal talents in trust and to use them for the service of society. 'To insist on more would be to kill the goose that laid the golden eggs.' If he owned a firm, a factory, or a large tract of land, he was to work alongside his employees, make profit by just means, pay decent wages, take no more than what he needed for a moderately comfortable life, plough the rest into his business or use it for worthwhile social purposes, involve his workers in decision making, and provide healthy working conditions and welfare schemes. For Gandhi such an economic arrangement had capitalists but not capitalism, socialism but not state ownership, and used capitalist managerial skills to achieve socialist purposes (M iii. 510–14).

Gandhi conceded that such a voluntary form of socialism or 'renunciation' was rare, and that only one of his many capitalist friends had come close to it. In his view the sustained pressure of educated and organized public opinion, including a *satyāgraha*, was the best way to establish trusteeship. If that did not work, he was reluctantly prepared to impose it by law. The law would prescribe the remuneration to be paid to the trustee 'commensurate with the service rendered and its value to society'. He was free to choose his heir, but the choice had to be finalized by the state. Gandhi thought that such a cooperative decision checked both. The trustee retained formal ownership of his property but his use of the profit, his income, and his choice of heir, were subject to state control. As Gandhi put it, 'I desire to end capitalism almost if not quite as much as the most advanced socialist and even communist. But our methods differ, our languages differ.' Gandhi's ideas on trusteeship were vague and underwent much revision. Despite his vacillations and confusions, he remained convinced that the two dominant forms of ownership, namely the capitalist and the communist, were both morally flawed, and that there had to be better alternatives. It is difficult to see how his idea of trusteeship could work in modern society, but it is not without historical parallels. Although it lacked an institutional form, it was to be found in the traditional Indian village community, and in different forms in classical Athens and Rome and the rural communities of medieval Europe.

For Gandhi economic life in a good society should not be autonomous and overbearing but embedded in and guided by moral considerations. A society's wealth consisted in the character of its members, not in the quantity of its material objects, and the purpose of its economic arrangements should be to create the necessary economic basis of the good life. This ensured that it had a sense of limit built into it and remained subject to collective human control.

All its adult members should work for their livelihood as a matter of both right and duty, the former because only through work could they develop their self-respect, initiative, capacity to cooperate with others, and self-discipline; the latter because work was one of the principal ways to contribute to social well-being and participate in the moral life of the community. Gandhi therefore thought it essential that every adult should have a guaranteed right to work. To deny it to him was to deny him both his right to moral self-development and the opportunity to discharge his social obligations. Welfare payments were a poor substitute for this, for while they sustained the body, they did nothing to develop moral and spiritual powers.

For reasons discussed earlier, Gandhi thought that human beings gained their full moral stature only in small, relaxed, and interdependent communities. Since the latter lacked vitality without an autonomous economic basis of their own, he argued that production should be decentralized and that each community should become relatively self-sufficient in its basic needs. As Gandhi imagined it, the village land was to be owned in common, farming done on a cooperative basis, the produce equitably divided, and only the surplus land used for cash crops. The villages were to encourage locally based industries and crafts, take pride in using local products, and import only what they could not themselves produce.

Since the village communities were to form the basic units of the economy, the nature, pace, and scale of industrialization were to be planned accordingly. Although large-scale industries were necessary, they should be restricted to the minimum, located in the cities, and only allowed to produce what the self-sufficient communities themselves could not. Since competition between them could easily lead to the present situation of unlimited production and widespread unemployment, it was to be strictly regulated. Gandhi was also worried about competition between the large urban-based industries and the village industries, which he thought would necessarily lead to the latter's destruction. A national plan was to be prepared, based on a detailed survey of what could be produced locally and what share of the market was to be reserved for this. This was the only way urban exploitation of the villages could be avoided. Gandhi was not opposed to machines but to *yantravād* (literally machinerism or indiscriminate mechanization), not to industry but to industrialism, and was deeply disturbed by the way in which greed-driven industrialization created mass unemployment, undermined human dignity, rendered people rootless, destroyed local communities, and caused moral and social havoc. He therefore advocated appropriate or intermediate technology, an ecologically safe mode of production, and a humanist or people-based rather than a product-based or consumerist economy.

Gandhi argued that, since the means of production of the basic necessities of life affected human survival and freedom and could easily lead to the most dangerous forms of exploitation, they should be owned by the state. It should either set them up itself or nationalize the existing ones. In the latter case, although the state should suitably reward their owners, it could not be expected to pay them a full market price, both because the industries were the products of collective communal effort and because the state could not raise the requisite money without imposing additional taxes on its citizens and thus 'robbing Peter to pay Paul'.

For Gandhi the state should lay down the minimum and maximum incomes. Since all socially useful activities were equally important, and since gross inequalities were morally corrupting and divisive, the income differential between them, necessary as it was because of human weakness, should be 'reasonable and equitable' and diminish over time. Gandhi thought that, once human beings came to see themselves as trustees of their talents and appreciated the value of a cohesive moral community, they would render their services out of a sense of pride and duty and find the incentive of higher incomes deeply offensive.

> If we are to be non-violent, we must not wish for anything on this earth which the meanest or the lowest of human beings cannot have.

The state

As we saw, Gandhi was deeply uneasy with the modern state. It was abstracted from society, centralized, bureaucratic, obsessed with homogeneity, and suffused with the spirit of violence. He thought that, since all the prevailing forms of government took the modern state for granted and represented different ways of organizing it, they were inherently incapable of tackling its structural defects. Even liberal democracy, the least objectionable of them all, did little to integrate state and society, decentralize political power, involve citizens in the conduct of public affairs, and reduce the extent and depth of internal and external violence. For Gandhi the vital task today was to explore alternatives not just to the contemporary forms of government but to the very institution of the state.

For Gandhi a society based on *swarāj*, a 'true democracy' as he called it, was the only morally acceptable alternative to the modern state. It was *shāsanmukta*, or free of domination and coercion, and institutionalized and nurtured *lokshakti*, or people's power. People here were, and knew themselves to be, the sole source of political power, and governed their affairs themselves. *Swarāj* involved not just the periodic accountability of government but the daily exercise of popular power, not just the enjoyment of civil and political rights but the constantly confirmed consciousness of being in charge of one's destiny, not just liberty but power (M iii. 235–75).

As Gandhi imagined it, the *swarāj*-based polity would be composed of small, cultured, well-organized, thoroughly regenerated, and self-governing village communities. Although he was not entirely clear on this point, he expected these communities to manage their local affairs themselves and to elect a small body of people to enforce their decisions. They would administer justice, maintain order, and take important economic decisions, and would be not merely administrative but powerful economic and political units. As such they would have a strong sense of solidarity, provide a genuine sense of community, and act as nurseries of civic virtues.

Beyond the relatively self-sufficient villages the country would be organized in terms of 'expanding circles'. The villages would be grouped into districts, these into provinces, and so on, each governed by representatives elected by its constituent units. Each tier of government would enjoy considerable autonomy and a strong sense of community, would both sustain and limit the one above it, and deal with matters of common interest to its constituent communities. Each province would draw up its own constitution to suit local requirements and in conformity with that of the country as a whole. The central government would wield enough authority to hold them all together, but not enough to dominate them. Gandhi was opposed to direct elections to the central assembly because they would be divisive and encourage corruption, and because the average voter was unlikely to be knowledgeable enough about the large issues of national policy to vote intelligently. The polity so constructed would not be a collection of isolated atoms but a 'community of communities', a unity of unities, a whole composed of wholes, a 'living organism' not an impersonal machine.

When a society consisted of different cultural and religious communities, Gandhi saw no need to homogenize them or even to subject them to a uniform system of laws. The attempt to do so was unnecessary, because cultural diversity not only did not undermine the unity of the state but gave it moral and cultural depth, and was also dangerous, because dismantling well-established communities was likely to provoke resistance and deprive their members of a sense of rootedness and power. Gandhi therefore insisted that the wider society should cherish its cultural communities and respect their languages, cultures, institutions, personal laws, and educational institutions. He agreed that some of their social practices might be morally offensive, but did not think that that justified government intervention. Coercion was generally evil, state intervention was bound to provoke resistance, and no practice could be eradicated without tackling its deeper moral roots. In Gandhi's view the offensive practices were best dealt with by the reformist campaigns of the enlightened members of the community concerned. Once they had discredited them and created the right climate, the law should consolidate and enforce the prevailing consensus.

Gandhi insisted that the state should be secular in the sense that it should not enforce, institutionalize, patronize, or financially support one or more religions. Religion was a personal though not a private matter. It had a deep social and political relevance, and hence religious discourse had its proper place in political life. While religion should enjoy respectable public presence and make its distinct contribution to the conduct of public affairs, the institutions of the state should in no way be associated with it. The state was concerned not with the quality of the human soul, which was best left in the care of the individual and society, but solely with secular or worldly interests. Gandhi was in favour of religious education in schools, and did not think that it detracted from the secular character of the state as long as all religions were taught in a 'spirit of reverence and broad-minded tolerance' and with a view to encouraging an inter-religious dialogue. In his view such education could create religious harmony and foster a climate of moral self-discipline, thereby decreasing the need for state coercion (M i. 450–1).

Since Gandhi disapproved of centralization and 'state worship', he suggested that many of the functions currently discharged by the state should be devolved on the local communities. One example will suffice to indicate what he had in mind. As a lawyer familiar with the modern system of administering justice, he was convinced that it was a most unfortunate and easily dispensable institution. It was expensive, dilatory, bureaucratic, and obsessed with uniformity. It treated human beings as passive objects in no way involved in the resolution of their conflicts and, despite its claim to get to the truth of the matter, privileged those capable of hiring the best lawyers.

Gandhi suggested that the local communities should become the centres of a radically redefined system of justice. Ideally they should encourage their members to settle their disputes themselves, and help create a moral climate in which to allow conflicts to occur or get out of control was widely regarded as a mark of personal inadequacy and a matter of shame. When conflicts could not be so resolved, local communities should provide people's courts made up of men and women enjoying widespread trust and respect. Acting as communal forums rather than as agencies of the state, the courts should be concerned not just with the administration of justice, for that left the roots of the conflicts untouched, but with the permanent resolution of underlying problems. And they should not just 'administer' justice as abstractly defined by the law, but help evolve more sensitive and individualized notions of justice by creatively interpreting the law in the light of the prevailing principles of social morality, natural justice, and common sense. Ideally they should aim not so much to apportion blame and punish the guilty as to restore the ruptured fabric of society, foster the spirit of goodwill and fair play, and increase the disputants' capacity to live together as members of a shared community.

In Gandhi's view such an arrangement would have many advantages over the present system of justice. Justice would be swift, inexpensive, easily intelligible, and dispensed without an elaborate judicial and legal establishment. The decisions reached would be grounded in the community's own system of values and carry greater moral authority. Since they would be based on the direct involvement of the parties concerned, they would be finely tuned to the complexity of the situation, fairer than at present, and would help raise the moral level of the community. Gandhi thought that if similar measures to integrate state and society and to encourage greater communal responsibility and initiative were to be introduced in other areas of life as well, the state would be transformed from an overbearing and central institution of society into its subordinate though obviously indispensable agency, interacting with others in a spirit of equal partnership and resorted to only when all else failed.

In Gandhi's view a truly democratic and non-violent society would not need the armed forces. It would have no aggressive designs on its neighbours. If it were attacked, it should rely on non-violent resistance. And if that failed and resulted in its conquest, it should rely on *satyāgraha*, including non-cooperation, to render the new government ineffective. Every government needed the support or at least the acquiescence of its subjects, and it would not last long if its united, determined, and non-violently trained subjects denied it all forms of active and passive support. Gandhi appreciated that this was an 'Euclidean' ideal but insisted that it was worth aiming at, and that in the meantime the best defence for a country was to rely on the combination of a small armed force and non-violently trained citizenry, supported by well-organized international economic and political pressure (xc. 503, 511; xxxvii. 271).

Gandhi felt the same way about the police. In his view armed police did not reduce crime but encouraged equally well-armed criminals, and generated a vicious cycle. Besides, crimes sprang from causes too deep to be tackled by the police. Ideally the community should become self-policing. Since that again was a 'Euclidean' ideal and since 'no government worth its name can suffer anarchy to prevail', the good society should establish a small and specialized police force (lxxi. 226).

The latter should carry only defensive weapons, be trained in non-violent methods of crowd control, work closely with the community, take on the role of social workers, and generally rely on their moral authority and the pressure of public opinion. They might become targets of criminal violence and even get killed. In Gandhi's view such martyrdom was likely to shake up the community, including the criminal, mobilize its moral energies, and over time reduce if not the extent, at least the level of criminal violence. In cases of large-scale riots and social disturbances, of which he had considerable experience, Gandhi argued that the police should be assisted by peace brigades made up of non-violently trained and locally or nationally respected citizens (lxxii. 403).

Gandhi was deeply troubled by the institution of the prison, where he had in all spent just under six years of his life. Prisons degraded and brutalized their inmates, were costly to run, absolved society of its responsibility for the causes of crimes, and so coarsened its moral sensibility that it saw nothing wrong in treating human beings as if they were wild animals to be kept in cages. For Gandhi, criminals were human beings endowed with the capacity to recognize evil and respond to good. To give up on any of them was an act of sacrilege and unworthy of a truly humane and non-violent society. Every act of crime signified a breakdown in the society's moral order, and both indicted and challenged it. Locking up the perpetrator was to lose an otherwise valuable member of society, incur the cost of his upkeep, and forfeit the opportunity to take a critical and constructive look at social institutions and practices.

In Gandhi's view, human beings committed crimes for a variety of reasons, such as poverty, a sense of injustice, lack of self-discipline, selfishness, and ill-will, and each required a sensitive response. If the crimes were caused by the first two, the community bore considerable responsibility for them and had a duty to tackle their roots. In other cases, the criminal bore much but not the whole of the responsibility. In such cases society should seek the support of the criminal's family, friends, neighbours, religious leaders, and the widely respected members of his community, and give them all the necessary help, encouragement, and incentive to reintegrate him into the community and develop in him the capacities for self-discipline, social concern, and moral responsibility. If that did not help, imprisonment might become necessary not so much to punish the criminal as to create an environment conducive to his moral reform. Ideally prisons should become workshops as well as educational and moral institutions, training criminals to become useful members of society in a humane environment and working closely with their families and friends to explore the forms of moral and social rehabilitation best suited to their individual needs. They would then cease to be brutal institutions operating on the dark margins of society and governed by practices considered intolerable in other institutions, and would instead become schools of reform subject to the same spirit of humanity that governed other areas of life (iii. 413; xiv. 1-6; xxiii. 508-12; xxiv. 224).

A citizen's responsibility

For Gandhi, neither consent nor will nor fear but cooperation was the basis of the state. Every state, democratic or otherwise, depended on the active or passive cooperation of its citizens. Since it was an agency of action, cooperation with it consisted in rendering it specific services such as carrying out its orders, paying taxes, fighting wars, and obeying laws. The state did not exist independently of its citizens, and was ultimately nothing more than a system of institutionalized cooperation between them.

Since the state was a vast and complex organization involving thousands of conscious and unconscious acts of daily cooperation by millions of citizens, they did not usually notice that they in fact sustained it and were morally responsible for its actions. And if they did, they excused themselves on the grounds that each of them was only an insignificant cog in a mighty wheel. Gandhi considered this a most dangerous fallacy. A mighty river was made up of individual drops, each of which contributed to its creation; the state was no different. Further, as a moral being every citizen had a duty to ask how he personally contributed to the maintenance of the state and whether he was happy about it. Citizens were responsible for their actions, and their responsibility was in no way diminished by what others did or failed to do.

Every government was tempted to misuse its power, and a democratic government was in that respect no better than an autocratic one. What distinguished the two was the fact that one did and the other did not succumb to the temptation. And this was so because, unlike the autocratic government, the democratic government knew that if it did succumb, its citizens would refuse to cooperate with it. Notwithstanding all its institutional checks and balances, a democratic government could easily turn evil if its citizens became apathetic or vulnerable to corruption and manipulation. The virtues and vices of a government were not inherent in it but derived from those of its citizens. As Gandhi put it:

> Rulers, if they are bad, are not so necessarily or wholly by reason of birth, but largely because of their environment. But the environment are we [*sic*] – the people who make the rulers what they are. They are thus an exaggerated edition of what we are in the aggregate . . . If we will reform ourselves, the rulers will automatically do so.

(M ii. 355)

As moral beings, citizens had a duty to decide to whom they should give their loyalty and support and under what conditions. Their self-respect and dignity required that their loyalty should not be unconditional or taken for granted. When a law was just, they had a 'sacred duty' to give it their 'willing and spontaneous obedience'. If it was unjust or morally unacceptable, they had the opposite duty. To obey it was to 'participate in evil' and incur moral responsibility for its consequences. It was a 'mere superstition' and an attitude worthy of a 'slave' to think that all laws, however unjust, deserved to be obeyed. Gandhi insisted that laws should not be judged in isolation from the general character of the state. If the state was intrinsically or mainly good, its occasional lapses should not be judged too harshly. No state was infallible and no one could be its member on his own terms.

For Gandhi, when citizens disobeyed a law, they should satisfy two conditions. First, their disobedience should be civil; that is, it should be public and non-violent, and they should show why they found the law unacceptable and should submit themselves to the prescribed punishment. Second, they should have earned the *adhikār* or moral right to disobey the law. Civil disobedience or non-cooperation with an otherwise good government was a serious matter with potentially grave consequences and required mature deliberation. Only those were entitled to resort to it, who had as a rule obeyed its laws, demonstrated their loyalty to the state, and proved their moral maturity by not turning every disagreement into an occasion for flaunting their consciences. When such otherwise law-abiding citizens disobeyed a law, their 'respectful disobedience' deserved a reasoned response. Rather than ruthlessly put them down, the government should appreciate that such acts nurtured the citizens' sense of moral responsibility and built up a vital moral capital that was bound to be useful to society in the long run. They also saved the government from falling all-too-easy prey to the temptation to abuse its power, and acted as a safety valve for popular discontent. Unlike an anarchist, who is 'an enemy of the state', such a civil resister is its 'friend' and his action is the 'purest type of constitutional agitation' (xx. 19).

Although Gandhi nowhere elaborated the criteria for evaluating the law, he thought that it was bad if it did one or more of the following. First, it was bad if it 'demeaned' and 'degraded' its subjects in their own or others' eyes, and required them to behave in a manner inconsistent with human dignity. Gandhi thought that the Nazi treatment of Jews and the white treatment of blacks in South Africa during his time there fell in this category. Second, a law was bad if it was patently partisan in its intent or outcome and discriminated against specific racial, religious, and other groups. And finally, a law was bad if it was repugnant to the vast majority of citizens and if opposition to it was universal. Its intrinsic merits, if any, were unimportant. The fact that it was passed in contempt of widespread opposition implied that the government treated its subjects with disdain. Such a law also involved a great deal of violence in the sense that most people either disobeyed it and had to be punished, or obeyed it out of fear of violence, and in either case it brought the state into disrepute.

Since majority rule violated the integrity of the minority and 'savoured of violence', and since unanimity was often impossible, all decisions in a non-violent society should be arrived at by rational discussion conducted in a spirit of goodwill and open-mindedness. For Gandhi rational discussion should avoid the rationalist fallacy mentioned earlier, and become not an exchange of arguments but an interpenetration of perspectives, a genuine fusion of minds and hearts. When that happened, the parties involved expanded each other's consciousness and range of sympathy, reconstituted each other's ways of looking at the world, and were reborn as a result of the encounter. In extreme cases, when no consensus was possible, the majority was to decide the matter after taking full account of minority views and strength of feeling, not because it was always right but because it was likely to be less mistaken or biased. If some citizens still felt deeply troubled by the decision, they were entitled to claim exemption from and in rare cases even to disobey it.

An assessment

Gandhi's vision of a non-violent society is informed by a powerful concern to place human beings at the centre of economic and political life, and contains many valuable insights. His emphases on the moral and cultural implications of the economic system, a humane process of production, sustainable development, a more balanced relation to nature, the right to gainful employment, and decentralized production are all well taken. So too are his imaginative explorations of new ways of reconstituting the state, new forms of state–society partnership, a non-violently constituted political order, humane ways of dealing with crime, a communally grounded system of justice, and politically responsible citizenship. Not surprisingly, many of these ideas have inspired new movements of thought not only in India but also elsewhere.

Gandhi's vision, however, suffers from several limitations. He postulates largely rural and self-sufficient village communities, and it is difficult to see how these are possible in a globally integrated economy, except on the naive assumption that a society can somehow turn its back on the rest of the world. The fact that Gandhi allows large-scale industries adds to his difficulties. It is naive to imagine that large-scale industries can be expected to remain confined to their officially allocated sphere, that they will respect the moral logic of the self-sufficient rural communities, that a national plan can neatly separate their respective spheres of operation, or that the two will not generate morally and economically incompatible ethos. This is not to deny that all this can be done, but rather that it requires a closed economy and a strong and authoritarian state, to both of which Gandhi was rightly opposed.

Gandhi's view of the state runs into similar difficulties. He was acutely aware of the need to eliminate poverty, reduce economic inequalities, ensure social justice, and to abolish such ugly social practices as untouchability. He appreciated that some large industries needed to be nationalized, and that the capitalists were unlikely to become trustees of their industries unless compelled to do so by the law. He also recognized that no polity could be held together unless its members shared a common sense of citizenship and saw themselves as *ekprajā* (a single people). It is difficult to see how all this can be achieved by a loosely structured and highly decentralized polity made up of largely autonomous communities whose members have limited contacts and share little in common. Taken together Gandhi's proposals require a fairly strong central government, an effective bureaucracy, a system of national planning, an institutional structure for articulating national public opinion, an internally articulated network of public spaces, and a coercive machinery to deal with the vested interests who might not be hospitable to Gandhi's idea of trusteeship. A polity with these and other features is not very different from the modern state.

Like many a moral idealist Gandhi found it difficult to appreciate the role of coercion in social life and come to terms with the state. He considered organized coercion to be inconsistent with human dignity, yet he could not avoid acknowledging that it was necessary to achieve the conditions for realizing, sustaining, and even generating the consciousness of human dignity. He condemned the state as an amoral and 'soul-less' machine, yet he could not deny that, as a vehicle for realizing worthwhile social goals, it was also moral in nature. While Gandhi was right to attack the statist political culture and explore new ways of mobilizing the individual and collective moral energies of its citizens, he was wrong to think that any modern community could dispense with the state altogether or make do with one that was weak, held in low esteem, and commanded little loyalty.

Chapter 7
Critical appreciation

Even five decades after Gandhi's death, opinions about his achievements remain deeply divided. For his critics he was too implacably hostile to modernity to offer an adequate understanding of its nature, let alone provide answers to its malaise. He was basically a man of action whose major contribution consisted in leading his country's struggle for independence. Some of his critics regard even this as a mixed legacy. In their view his basically conservative, puritanical, pro-bourgeois, and pacifist thought hindered the development of radical political movements, harmed the long-term interests of the *dalits* (formerly untouchables), burdened the Indian psyche with a sense of guilt about economic development, hampered the emergence of a strong and powerful state, and perpetuated unrealistic and confused ideas about human sexuality. His introduction of religious language into politics alienated the Muslims and rendered the partition of the country unavoidable. And his flawed strategy of national regeneration failed to develop the conventional forms of institutional politics, especially the ideologically based political parties that independent India badly needed and in whose absence its political life suffered grave damage.

Gandhi's admirers take a radically different view. For them he was a man of both thought and action, a rare combination. As a man of thought, he saw through the madness of modernity, and offered an alternative vision that combined the best insights of both the pre-modern and modern world-views while avoiding the self-indulgent individualism and moral complacency of the currently fashionable post-modernism. He also discovered a uniquely moral method of political change in the form of *satyāgraha*, and provided an effective alternative to violence. As a man of action he led the greatest anti-colonial struggle in history, encouraged a humane and liberal form of patriotism, showed how to lead a successful political life without compromising one's integrity, and offered a rare example of morally responsible leadership. Christian commentators, who suggestively have long compared him to and even seen him as the twentieth-century version of Jesus Christ, argue that he was the first man in history to show how to relate religion and politics without corrupting either and to give political life a much-needed spiritual basis. Some of Gandhi's admirers go even further and contend that we should not be surprised if one day he were to prove as influential and be placed on the same footing as Jesus Christ and the Buddha.

Although Gandhi's detractors and admirers make some valid points, they evaluate both him and his legacy in somewhat superficial terms. He was certainly a creative thinker, a political leader, a social reformer, a deeply religious person, and so on, and in each role he had his strengths and weaknesses, some of which were indicated in earlier chapters. Gandhi, however, also operated at a much deeper level, and to ignore that is to miss out what was distinctive to him.

The vision of non-violence

All his adult life Gandhi sought to articulate and live out an original and powerful vision of human existence. As we have seen, he was deeply troubled by violence in all its crude and subtle forms, and passionately yearned to lead a life of true non-violence. He wondered if and how it was possible to be profoundly at peace with oneself, other human beings, and with one's natural and social environment, how to live without hurting and harming a single living being and even wishing to

"THE ODD THING ABOUT ASSASSINS, DR. KING, IS THAT THEY THINK THEY'VE KILLED YOU."

6. 'The odd thing about assassins . . .' Cartoon by Mauldin from the *Chicago Sun-Times*, 1968

do so. He relentlessly explored the logic of that vision, sincerely tried to live it, and experimented with ways to overcome the inevitable obstacles.

Since mankind had long accepted violence as the inescapable basis of life and organized its affairs on the opposite vision to his, Gandhi was led to ask the deepest and most searching questions about the traditional ways of thought and life. He asked why human beings thought they had a right to exploit nature and use other living beings for their purposes. He asked why there should be such a coercive institution as the state, indeed why human beings should be subjected to coercion at all when it so clearly violated their dignity, and what kind of society would eliminate the need for it. He felt deeply troubled about the armed forces, the police, the prisons, and the wars, all of which seemed to him an affront to human dignity and indicative of a profound failure of moral and political imagination. He felt no less troubled by the violence and dehumanization of both capitalism and communism, and asked if there was a more moral way of organizing the economy.

Gandhi carried his search for non-violence into the realm of the human mind itself, and asked how one should relate to one's thoughts, beliefs, and feelings in a truly non-violent manner. It was important to co-ordinate and harmonize one's ideas, but to systematize them into a neat and logically coherent theory was to do violence both to the inherently fluid world of experience and to the inescapably tentative process of thinking itself. It was necessary to hold firm beliefs and pass judgements on individuals and situations, but one needed to ensure that these did not do violence to the inherent ambiguity of the subject matter or to other ways of looking at it. A sense of identity – personal, religious, political, and so on – was important, but it should not be defined in rigid, static, and exclusive terms as it then did psychological and even physical violence to those excluded by it as well as suppressed and did violence to its own internal plurality. Gandhi wondered how identity could be determinate without becoming rigid, give one a sense of rootedness without turning it into a prison, create a sense of boundary without making it a barrier to dialogue.

Thanks to his passionate commitment to a non-violent vision of human life, Gandhi challenged conventional wisdom, broke through traditional categories of thought, stretched the boundaries of imagination in all areas of life, and opened up new philosophical and practical possibilities. Gandhi's questions demand answers. And if we reject his answers, as we are bound to do in several cases, we need to provide alternative answers. He requires us to think afresh about things we have long taken for granted, and therein lies his greatest contribution and true originality.

Gandhi's vision was intensely moralistic, and yet it remained remarkably free from the utopianism, romanticism, fanaticism, and despair that have often shadowed moralism. This was so because he took great care to ensure that his vision was not itself pervaded by the spirit of violence. He did not think of it as an ideal to realize but as a moral compass with which to navigate one's way through life. He also made ample allowance for the fact that different individuals were bound to interpret and articulate the vision differently, and thus avoided dogmatism and fanaticism. Gandhi's vision was also sensitive to the limitations of the human condition, and encouraged compromise and accommodation. It was striking that when his countrymen disappointed him, as they did during periods of intercommunal violence, he did not become bitter, condemn them for not being worthy of him and his ideals, despair of them, or withdraw from the scene. He persisted in his task, patiently appealed to them, rebuked but rarely blamed them, never flew into a rage or felt self-righteous and superior, and generally succeeded in evoking the desired response.

As for the content of Gandhi's vision, it had its strengths and limitations. He rightly argued that human beings were interdependent in ways they did not often appreciate, and that in brutalizing and degrading others they brutalized and degraded themselves as well. This led to a fascinating theory of social criticism and change. He showed that victims of injustices were never totally innocent, that an unjust system took its toll on both its victims and alleged beneficiaries, and that it was in the interest of both to change it. Rather than polarize the battle against injustice and place the onus of struggle on its victims, Gandhi's view turned it into a shared moral task to which all alike had a duty to contribute.

Such a view runs the risk of degenerating into a sentimental and politically naive humanism attacking such vague and abstract targets as 'the system' or 'the evil in the human heart'. Gandhi avoided that mistake. Since the dominant groups upheld and benefited from an unjust system, they formed the *immediate* targets of struggle and had to be fought. However, since not they personally but the system was the real source of injustice, it was the *ultimate* target of attack. Unlike sentimental humanists Gandhi identified enemies and knew whom to fight against, but unlike conventional revolutionary theorists he also saw them as victims and hence as potential partners in a common emancipatory struggle. Gandhi's thought thus had room for both indignation and love, both struggle and cooperation. This enabled him to stress the unity of means and ends, the moral dimension of politics, and a non-Manichean and cooperative view of political struggle, all of which lay at the basis of his remarkable theory of *satyāgraha*.

Transcending liberalism

Gandhi's vision enabled him to articulate an impressive moral and political theory that combines the important insights of both liberalism and communitarianism. Like liberals he stressed freedom but defined it very differently. For him freedom consisted in being true to oneself, in living by one's own light and growing at one's own pace, and represented a form of wholeness or integrity. It involved knowing and accepting oneself as one was, recognizing one's limits and possibilities, and making choices on the basis of that knowledge. If my way of life suited me, enabled me to do what I wanted to do, and I was content with it, I did not cease to be free simply because I had not chosen it. Freedom did not consist in choice *per se*, as some liberals argue, nor in making choices considered to be *higher*, as the idealists argue, but in making choices that were in harmony with and capable of being integrated into one's way of life. It had nothing to do with the *number* of alternatives available to the agent either. If these alternatives did not include what one needed, they had no significance. And if what one needed was the only choice available, the absence of others in no way diminished one's freedom. Gandhi subsumed freedom under truth and offered a novel way of defending it. Only the free man, that is, one able to make his choices and decisions himself, was able to discover, develop, and live by his unique ontological truth. Freedom was thus the necessary basis and precondition of one's ability to be true to oneself. To deny a man freedom was to force him to be untrue to himself and to live by someone else's truth. For Gandhi the case for freedom was the same as that for truthfulness.

Even as Gandhi radically redefined the concept of freedom, he redefined the concept of equality. In much of the liberal and socialist literature on the subject, equality is defined in comparative, contractual, competitive, and individualist terms. Gandhi argued that human beings were necessarily interdependent, rose and fell together, and were born subject to non-repayable debts. Since society was necessarily a fellowship of unique and interdependent beings, the concept of equality had to be defined in non-comparative, non-competitive, and non-atomistic terms. In Gandhi's view it basically consisted in each individual enjoying full access to his or her community's economic, political, moral, and cultural resources in order to realize his or her unique potential, not an abstract human potential as determined by a philosophical conception of human nature or by an arbitrary moral standard but their potential as *uniquely constituted beings*.

As progressive and reflective beings individuals 'grew from truth to truth' and strove to enrich, deepen, and reconstitute their being. Equality consisted in all alike being able to do so. It did not mean that I should get what others get, but rather that I should get what I need for my development. And it was not only in my interest but in that of all others that they should treat me equally, for in degrading and demeaning me they degraded and demeaned themselves as well and deprived themselves of the contribution I would make as a rich human being. Equality thus was not a narrowly individualistic concept or a synonym for uniformity. It was at bottom a relationship of mutuality and fellowship.

Gandhi also redefined the concepts of right and duty. Like liberals he valued rights, but he insisted that they were inseparable from duties and needed to be defined and exercised in a socially responsible manner. He stressed the importance of justice, but insisted that it was not the highest value and became legalistic, competitive, and narrowly distributivist unless grounded in and energized and limited by the larger values of human fellowship and solidarity. Like liberals he valued tolerance, but unlike them he insisted that it was condescending and judgemental and needed to be replaced by a logically and morally more satisfactory concept of goodwill. Gandhi similarly redefined the concept of citizenship, and stressed the ideas of political participation, self-discipline, concern for others, and personal responsibility that are often ignored in liberal writings.

Gandhi also sketched the outlines of a highly suggestive non-rationalist theory of rationality. Although he took a rather narrow view of reason, he rightly argued that it was not the only valuable or even the highest human faculty. This enabled him to cherish and champion faculties, modes of cognition, forms of knowledge, and styles of reasoning and discourse that are often devalued in a narrowly positivist world-view, and to create a theoretical and moral space for traditions, intuition, collective wisdom, and feelings. Gandhi's view that each civilization, religion, and way of life had its strengths and limitations enabled him to highlight both the possibility and the necessity of an intercultural dialogue, and to argue that learning and borrowing from other traditions in no way compromised one's loyalty to one's own. As we have seen, he himself freely borrowed ideas from different traditions, brought them into a creative interplay, and arrived at new ones that none of these traditions alone could have generated on its own.

His concept of *satyāgraha* is a good example of this. It has resonance in both Hindu and Christian religious traditions, but it has never been a part of either. It is basically composed of three important ideas, namely the spiritual nature of human beings, the power of suffering love, and the skilful use of the latter to reach out to and activate the moral energies of others. The first metaphysical belief is common to both Hinduism and Christianity and indeed to all other religions; the ontology of suffering love is unique to Christianity, and Gandhi himself said that he borrowed it from the latter: the idea that the 'soul' is energy, that two 'souls' can directly communicate by non-lingual means, and that they can influence and activate each other is an important part of Hindu epistemology and informs complex forms of yoga. Since by and large Christianity lacks the third, and Hinduism the second element, one needed to be deeply familiar with both traditions in order to arrive at anything resembling the Gandhian concept of *satyāgraha*.

Limitations

While highlighting some of the neglected dimensions of human existence, Gandhi's intensely moralistic vision also blinded him to several others. He either ignored or took a dim view of the intellectual, scientific, aesthetic, sensuous, and other aspects of life. He rarely saw a film, read a book of poetry, visited an art gallery, watched a game, or took any interest in history, archaeology, modern science, wildlife, unspoilt nature, and India's natural beauty. This was not because he was intellectually incurious, for he showed remarkable experimental vitality in the matters that most interested him, but because his moralistic vision prevented him from seeing the significance of these and other activities. When the discovery of the North Pole was announced, he wondered what good it had done to the world and why it should arouse excitement. When he visited the Vatican museum, he briskly swept past Botticelli's and Michelangelo's frescos, but stood motionless and wept before a painting of the crucifixion. For Gandhi the care of the soul was a full-time job requiring undivided attention, and the arts and sciences were relevant only to the extent that they promoted that supreme goal. Such a single-minded view of life naturally generated enormous energy and enabled him to explore moral and spiritual life in great depth and without distraction, but it also led to the devaluation of other human pursuits and forms of excellence and to the lack of a critical and wider perspective on the nature and relative significance of the moral and spiritual life itself.

Gandhi's view of human life made it difficult for him to explain and come to terms with evil. For him good was real, positive, self-subsistent, omnipotent, whereas evil was epiphenomenal, negative, parasitic upon and only made possible by the absence or weakness of the good. Since his thought did not prepare him for evil, he was constantly puzzled by it. With his long experience of fighting against injustices, he obviously knew better than most that human beings could be selfish, dogmatic, prejudiced, self-righteous, but not that they could also be 'brutes' or 'savages'. His theory of human nature could only explain savagery as a temporary loss of humanity capable of being set right by an appropriate surgery of the soul. When he was confronted with the depth and extent of intercommunal brutality, he felt morally disoriented and could not make sense of it. As we saw, he fought an extraordinarily courageous battle against it, but his victories were temporary, lacked institutional permanence, and remained heavily dependent on his increasingly declining charisma and the diminishing goodwill of his morally overstretched countrymen.

Like many religious idealists, Gandhi had great difficulty in understanding the nature and role of force and violence in human affairs. For him physical force was always evil and could at best have only a limited prudential justification. That was why he refused to accept that the state could be a moral institution, or that its use of force could serve moral purposes. He had similar difficulties with violence. For him non-violence never failed; if it did, it was not pure enough and the fault lay with its agent. As Gandhi grew older, his views began to change. He saw that the state could be an instrument of social justice and equality, and that it needed the armed forces. And he also saw that violence was sometimes not only practically unavoidable but also moral, and needed to be judiciously combined with non-violence in a balanced theory of social change. However, these concessions were *ad hoc*, tentative, grudging, and not fully integrated into his theories of the state and non-violence. While his practice showed much realism, his theories remained 'Euclidean' or idealistic, exposing him to the mistaken but understandable charge of hypocrisy, as when he condoned violence during the Quit India movement of 1942 and gave his 'tacit consent' to the dispatch of Indian troops to Kashmir in 1947. Rather than insist on a pure theory and permit impure practices, the more sensible thing would have been to legitimize and regulate the latter by making space for them within the theory itself.

Gandhi's impoverished view of human life prevented him from appreciating the central principles and internal dialectic of modern civilization. His critique of it made many telling points and exposed its racist, imperialist, violent, and irrational underside, but it also missed out and distorted a good deal. He took little account of its commitment to the values of equality, individuality, critical self-reflection, and social justice, its passionate desire to understand and master natural and social forces, its restless search for a better society, and the way in which it has brought different civilizations and cultures together and made them a universally accessible human resource. Even the ideas of universal love and indivisible humanity, which Gandhi rightly cherished, are inconceivable outside the interdependent world made possible by modern civilization. Gandhi's emphasis on the human need for roots and the value of small communities is well taken, but his local communities are too isolated and self-contained to be realistic and too parochial and self-absorbed to avoid becoming moral prisons. Small communities built behind the back of and in relative contempt of modern civilization are quite different in nature from those that enjoy full access to and delight in drawing upon its diverse resources. Gandhi was too realistic not to see this and kept modifying his views. But his heart hankered after the simplicity of rural life and remained in tension with his head.

Life

We turn finally to Gandhi's life, his only 'real book' as he called it and by which alone he wished to be judged. It had a rare sweep and grandeur. There have been greater saints, religious and social reformers, spiritual seekers, moralists, statesmen, nationalist leaders, and organizers than he, but it is difficult to think of one who was all these and fought simultaneously on so many fronts with varying degrees of success. For the first 30 odd years of his life he dutifully obeyed the conventions of his society and married, raised children, and discharged his social obligations. Thereafter his life underwent a profound change and was dominated by a Buddha-like passion for *moksha*. As we saw, *moksha* meant three things to him: first, complete mastery of all the senses including sexuality; second, a totally pure and transparent mind freed of fear, jealousy, pettiness, meanness, vanity, and other base passions; and third, dissolution of the sense of selfhood by becoming one with all living beings in a spirit of universal love and service. Although the first two related to the personal and the third to the social and political areas of life, the separation was purely notional and ultimately incoherent for Gandhi. The search for moral purity when dissociated from an active concern for others was self-centred and ultimately a form of self-indulgence; the reverse signified a moral busybody and a form of escapism. For Gandhi one had to seek one's perfection not outside but within the world, not away from but in the midst of struggles against injustices, inequalities, oppression, and other evils.

While carrying on great campaigns against racism in South Africa, British rule in India, and the injustices of his own society, Gandhi also continued his struggle to become as pure and diaphanous as a human being could be. He identified his moral and spiritual limitations and set about overcoming them one by one. In his case the success did not come in a sudden act of illumination or grace, such as sometimes transforms a person's life overnight, but after a painful and protracted struggle. Over time he conquered his great love of food, easily aroused anger, arrogance, a strong streak of vanity, selfishness, possessiveness, jealousy, personal attachments, physical cowardice, and personal ambition, and increasingly became spiritually 'lighter'. Sex had obsessed him in his early adolescence, and he strove not just to suppress or even master it but totally to eliminate it in his pursuit of 'absolute' innocence. We have already seen what that involved. The struggles at all levels were fierce and marked by moments of deep self-doubt and despair, but he persisted and fashioned a life which, though narrow in its focus and not altogether free of human limitations, had an enormous depth and a rare moral and spiritual beauty.

Four random incidents of his remarkable life reveal the nobility of the soul he crafted and the great virtues he cultivated. During one of his many periods of incarceration, a black warder was bitten by a scorpion. When Gandhi heard his screams, he rushed to the spot, called for a doctor, and in the meantime started sucking out the poisoned blood, without the slightest thought for his life and in utter disregard of his own bleeding gums caused by dental surgery just a few days before. He went on spitting out the sucked blood until the victim felt relief, and was gone before the latter and others had a chance to thank him.

Indulal Yajnik, his one-time colleague and a prominent socialist, turned

7. Gandhi's worldly possessions

against him and wrote a vicious attack on him. He regretted this later and went to Gandhi to apologize. It was Gandhi's day of silence. He saw Yajnik among his visitors and before the latter could say anything greeted him with a reassuring smile, and sent him a hastily scribbled note complimenting him for changing his views only once whereas he, Gandhi, had done so far more often. Poor Yajnik was in tears.

As we have seen, he rose to incredible heights during the years of intercommunal violence and staked everything in his fight against it. He did so for two related reasons (B 372–82). His entire life had been based on the passionate conviction that soul-force or non-violence was infinitely more powerful than brute force, and he felt that he had to prove its truth. He also seems to have thought that he could perhaps have handled Hindu–Muslim relations differently, that he had made mistakes, that he bore some responsibility for the violence, and that it was his *dharma* to fight and atone for it. Gandhi vastly exaggerated his share of responsibility and was excessively harsh on himself. However, for someone with his conscience and standards of self-evaluation, even the smallest error of judgement required penance. It is difficult to think of many higher examples of morally sensitive political leadership.

Maulana Azad, the Congress President in 1946, had, without Gandhi's knowledge and against his considered view, sent Stafford Cripps, the visiting British minister, a confidential note saying that he and the Congress had an open mind on the partition of India. When Cripps called on Gandhi, he was surprised to find that latter knew nothing about the note, and left it with him to mull over. When Azad went to see Gandhi the next day, Gandhi asked him if there was any communication between him and Cripps. Azad told a lie. Although his note to Cripps was lying on Gandhi's desk, Gandhi kept quiet. After Maulana's depature Gandhi's secretary copied out the note for future use. Gandhi rebuked him, asked him to tear up the copy and return the original to

Cripps, and blamed himself for being unworthy of Maulana's trust!

> A man of wisdom and humility, armed with resolve and inflexible consistency, who has devoted all his strength to the uplifting of his people and the betterment of their lot; a man who has confronted the brutality of Europe with the dignity of the simple human being and thus at all times risen superior.
>
> Generations to come, it may be, will scarce believe that such a one as this ever in flesh and blood walked upon this earth.
>
> Einstein on Gandhi

Glossary

adhikār a right; a right that is earned or deserved

advaita non-dualism, monism

ahimsā non-violence, absence of a desire to harm a living being

anāsakti non-attachment

āshram a commune of spiritual aspirants organized around a guru

ātman soul or spirit

buddhi intelligence

chetanā consciousness

dalits those previously untouchables. The untouchables were people considered so low as to be placed outside the pale of normal physical contact

dharma duty, moral law, characteristic activity of a class of objects or beings

ekprajā a sense of belonging to a single community

fakir Muslim ascetic or mendicant

hartāl cessation of work as an expression of protest

karma action, law of moral retribution

khādi hand-spun cloth

lokshakti people's power, power generated by people's collective action

Mahātma great soul. An honorific title conferred on Gandhi by Rabindranath Tagore

maitri friendliness

manas mind

moksha liberation, release from the cycle of rebirth

nishkām karma disinterested action

sadbhāva goodwill, a wish to see someone flourish

satya truth

satyāgraha non-violent resistance

satyāgrahi one who engages in non-violent resistance

shakti energy or power

shāsanmukta free of domination or coercive rule

sukṣma ṣarira non-material 'body' or configuration that accompanies an individual through his successive lives

swabhāva distinct psychological and moral constitution of each individual

swarāj self-rule, individual or collective autonomy

tapas penance

ulema Muslim theologian

untouchables see dalits

yajna any activity undertaken in the spirit of sacrifice to a deity

yantravād mechanization as an end in itself or for its own sake

Bibliographical background

Men of action are generally too busy or discreet to write about their thoughts and experiences except after their retirement, and sometimes not even then. Yet the writings of Gandhi, who led an unusually active life, fill 90 volumes and even they are incomplete! The fact that he enjoyed leisure during the just under six years that he spent in prison provides only a small part of the explanation, for much of his writing was not done in prison. The deeper explanation is to be found in the way he defined action and the kind of active life he led. Action for him was intended not so much to achieve certain results as to live out a specific way of life, which he naturally needed to explain to his countrymen. Besides, the way of life could not be worked out in advance, and hence his whole life became one long series of 'experiments'. It is striking that the word 'experiment' occurs frequently in Gandhi's writings and that he called his autobiography *Experiments with Truth or Autobiography*. Since the meaning and implications of his experiments were not always clear to him or to others, he had to write about them. As he wrote, he evoked strong responses, to which he had to respond. For Gandhi writing thus became inseparable from action. He was therefore never too busy to write because writing was an integral part of his business.

Gandhi's ideas are to be found in two kinds of writings, those written by him and by his close associates and secretaries. Gandhi's own writings consist of seven books; numerous articles and editorials in the four weekly journals that he edited at various times in his life; interviews, some of them long and probing, with journalists and foreign visitors; letters to his perplexed associates, followers, and total strangers; and important speeches at various religious, cultural, and political meetings. Most of these are included in the 90 volumes of his *Collected Works*. Gandhi's seven books include *Hind Swarāj*, *Satyāgraha in South Africa*, *Autobiography*, *Constructive Programme: Its Meaning and Place*, *Discourses on the Gita*, *Āshram Observances in Action*, and *A Guide to Health*, all published by Navajivan, Ahmedabad.

Gandhi's secretaries and associates have published several volumes describing his day-to-day activities and conversations with them and visitors. Among these Pyarelal's *Mahātma Gandhi: The Early Phase*, Vol. 1, and *The Last Phase*, Vol. 1, Books 1 and 2 (Ahmedabad, 1956) are the best. They largely deal with younger and older Gandhi's social and political thought and activities. For intimate insights into his inner struggles and views about individuals, events, and life in general, the best accounts are 15 volumes of Mahadev Desai's posthumously published *Diary* (Ahmedabad, 1960–74), and two volumes of Manuben Gandhi's *Delhima Gandhiji* (Ahmedabad, 1964 and 1966) sadly not yet translated into English. Both of them wrote in Gujarati, their own and Gandhi's native language. Manu Gandhi was Gandhi's great-niece, and Mahadev Desai, his secretary from 1917 to 1942, was in Gandhi's own words 'more than a son' to him.

Gandhi wrote most of his books in his native Gujarati partly as a matter of principle, partly to develop the language, and partly to show how other Indian languages should be written. Since their English translations were done in a hurry and since he only checked a couple and that rather too quickly, they are generally unreliable. The English translations of Mahadev Desai's works by V. G. Desai are no better. Since hardly any foreign commentator and only a few Indian commentators seem to read Gujarati, their works remain flawed. For a fuller discussion of this, see my 'Gandhi and his Translators', *Gandhi Marg*, June 1986.

There is no plan to retranslate Gandhi's or his close associates' writings, and that is a big handicap to Gandhi scholars with no knowledge of Gujarati. I have relied on the Gujarati originals and corrected the translations when necessary. A. Parel, ed. *Hind Swarāj* (Cambridge, 1997) is the best translation of Gandhi's seminal work with a valuable introduction.

Biography

Gandhi has been the subject of over 20 biographies and over 25 biographical sketches in English. The first one, by his friend Revd Joseph J. Doke, *M. K. Gandhi: An Indian Patriot in South Africa* (London, 1909), is of considerable historical value because it was written with Gandhi's co-operation and before he became a world figure. Many subsequent biographies were written by journalists who met and stayed with him for different lengths of time. Among them Louis Fischer's two books cited in the Abbreviations are the best. One of the most recent and impressive biographies is by Judith Brown, cited in the Abbreviations.

No biography of Gandhi so far has been able fully to capture and illuminate the complexity, tensions, and apparent contradictions of his personality, or to elucidate the sources of his powerful emotional hold over so many of his associates as well as his countrymen in general. This is not surprising, for a good biographer would need to be fully familiar with all the major religious traditions that shaped him, master Gujarati, and possess a deep intuitive understanding of the social and cultural milieu in which he grew up. And even then the biographer would suffer from the disadvantage of not having reliable biographies of Gandhi's closest associates including his wife, Mahadev Desai, Miraben and Manu Gandhi. It is striking that many of his biographers are Christians and that few Indian scholars so far have attempted a major biography based on primary sources in South Africa and elsewhere.

Further reading

Thought

For Gandhi's philosophical and religious thought, see Margaret Chatterjee, *Gandhi's Religious Thought* (London, 1983), R. Iyer, *The Moral and Political Thought of Mahātma Gandhi* (New York, 1973), and B. Parekh, *Colonialism, Tradition and Reform* (Delhi, 1999). For Gandhi's moral and political thought, see R. Iyer, *The Moral and Political Thought of Mahātma Gandhi* (New York, 1973), B. Parekh, *Gandhi's Political Philosophy* (London, 1989), and R. Terchek, *Gandhi: Struggling for Autonomy* (Lanham, 1998).

Gandhi's non-violence and *satyāgraha* have rightly attracted much attention. For good discussions, see J. Bondurant, *Conquest of Violence* (Berkeley, 1965), G. Sharp, *Gandhi Wields the Weapon of Moral Power* (Ahmedabad, 1960) and *The Politics of Nonviolent Action* (Boston, 1973), and D. Dalton, *Mahātma Gandhi: Nonviolent Power in Action* (Columbia, NY, 1993). For a good study of whether and how Gandhi's method could have been applied by the German Jews, see Gideon Shimoni, *Gandhi, Satyāgraha and the Jews* (Jerusalem, 1977). The book analyses Gandhi's correspondence with Jewish writers and relations with his Jewish friends. H. Raines, *My Soul is Rested* (New York, 1983) discusses the effect of the Salt March on the imagination of African Americans. For a good discussion of Gandhi's influence on African Americans, see S. Kapur, *Raising up a Prophet: The African American Encounter with Gandhi* (Boston, 1992).

For Gandhi's controversial experiments in celibacy, see N. K. Bose, *My Days with Gandhi* (Delhi, 1974) and B. Parekh, *Colonialism, Tradition and Reform* (Delhi, 1999). This was once an extremely sensitive subject. As Bose explains in the preface, Navajivan, Gandhi's official publisher, refused to publish his book, while I was attacked as 'Hindu Rushdie' and faced some opposition. The fact that the opposition soon died down and that no harm was threatened to me suggests that this is now an accepted area of investigation. To cover it adequately would require access to the diaries of Manu, one of the women involved in Gandhi's experiments. The diaries do seem to exist and were last seen in 1963, but their current whereabouts are unknown. The other women, all now dead, did not keep diaries, but accounts of their conversations with others on the subject do exist.

For short and balanced accounts of Gandhi's life, work, and thought, see A. Copley, *Gandhi* (London, 1987) and D. Rothermund, *Mahātma Gandhi* (Delhi, 1991). For a critical study of the recent commentaries on Gandhi's political thought and role, see Thomas Pantham, *Political Theories and Social Reconstruction: A Critical Survey of the Literature on India* (Delhi 1995). Given Gandhi's habits, dress, and intriguing personality, he became the subject of countless cartoons, which give a good idea of how his baffled British contemporaries tried to make sense of him. For an excellent collection, see *Gandhi in Cartoons* (Ahmedabad, 1970).

Index

Page numbers in *italics* refer to illustrations.

Expand your collection of
VERY SHORT INTRODUCTIONS